The FOUNDATIONS of FREEDOM

*The Interrelationship Between
Democracy and Human Rights*

The
FOUNDATIONS
of
FREEDOM

The Interrelationship Between
Democracy and Human Rights

DURWARD V. SANDIFER
and
L. RONALD SCHEMAN

FOREWORD BY JOSÉ A. MORA

FREDERICK A. PRAEGER, *Publishers*
New York · Washington · London

FREDERICK A. PRAEGER, PUBLISHERS
111 Fourth Avenue, New York, N.Y. 10003, U.S.A.
77–79 Charlotte Street, London W.1, England

Published in the United States of America in 1966
by Frederick A. Praeger, Inc., Publishers

Library of Congress Catalog Card Number: 65-24934

Printed in the United States of America

Foreword

One of the concerns that has been constantly expressed at meetings of the Organization of American States is the need to clarify the relationship between respect for human rights and the effective exercise of representative democracy. It is obvious that this concern was in the minds of the men who drafted the Charter of Bogotá, for it declares that "the solidarity of the American states and the high aims which are sought through it require the political organization of those states on the basis of the effective exercise of representative democracy."

Article 13 of the Charter, moreover, in recognizing the right of states to develop freely and naturally their cultural, political, and economic life, provides that it is the duty of the state to respect the rights of the individual. It follows, therefore, that by the terms of the Charter respect for human rights is a contractual obligation to which the governments have formally subscribed. To this may be added the moral weight of the American Declaration of the Rights and Duties of Man and the Universal Declaration of the United Nations. The Ninth International Conference of American States, in approving the first-mentioned declaration, stated that "juridical and political institutions, which regulate life in human society, have as their principal aim the protection of the essential rights of men."

It is of prime importance that the various points deriving from the principles adopted by the inter-American system be clarified so that there may be an effective advance in application of the standards governing the life of our regional community.

Professor Durward V. Sandifer, a distinguished member of the Inter-American Commission on Human Rights, and L. Ronald Scheman here approach the subject with unquestionable authority. Their study is of greatest value, in that it results from practical working experience with a body charged —among other duties—with stimulating a human-rights consciousness in the peoples of America and with making recommendations to the governments for the adoption, within the framework of domestic legislation, of progressive measures leading to more faithful observance of those rights. The authors' presentation leads one to a conviction that the establishment of strict safeguards to human rights is an essential prerequisite to the effective operation of democracy.

In the last analysis, democracy is but the orderly regulation of liberty. The treatise by Dr. Sandifer and Mr. Scheman has the merit of seeking to strike a balance between doctrinaire principle and the practical application thereof. On the basis of such a balance a democratic system could be evolved which would permit of meeting our peoples' continuous demands for change in legal fashion. The practice of democracy is the best means of ensuring that the constant upward movement of the community will attain its goal.

Following an excellent analysis of civil and political rights, this study finally treats, with clarity and penetration, one of the most delicate points of the present problem: the role to be played by international organizations when they enter into matters traditionally reserved to the domestic jurisdiction of the several states. Progress is being made in this field, thanks to the application of international standards freely agreed upon by the states in full exercise of their sovereignty. In this respect, activities of international cooperation, undertaken with the assent of the states, may, by stimulating political education and the development of the regional community, lead to the triumph of the principles and to the achievement of the goals set forth in the instruments of the inter-American system. "The international protection of the rights of man should be the principal guide of an evolving American law," the Bogotá Conference declared in 1948.

A profound faith in democracy is the sole guarantee of respect for human rights. The contribution of Dr. Sandifer and Mr. Scheman seems to me to have come at a timely moment for consolidating doctrine that has been developed in a variety of instruments to which the nations of America have subscribed—instruments whose effective operation throughout the Hemisphere can be ensured only by persevering action on the part of all.

José A. Mora, *Secretary General*
Organization of American States

Preface

This book has been written with one specific purpose: to provide a concise explanation of the fundamental reasons for the necessity for the democratic form of government and for respect for human rights. Of course, this task has been attempted many times in the past, in many forms, by statesmen, political scientists, and philosophers of first rank. One may wonder, then, why we should wish to add another chapter to testimony already distinguished for its scholarship and depth of analysis. There are two reasons. First, although much has been written about human rights, and even more has been said about democracy, surprisingly little has been written explicitly relating the two to each other. It is our purpose to demonstrate, in a practical and pragmatic manner, why a strict regard for human rights is essential to democracy and, conversely, why the democratic form of government alone ensures the observance of those fundamental rights. These two great ideas of man are inseparable. An understanding of their relationship is urgent in this modern world, where all sorts of theories and systems are constantly pressed upon an anxious public by would-be saviors of humanity.

The second reason is that, although much has been written on these subjects, and many eulogies are glibly passed off in public pronouncements, explanations of the rationale and purposes of the democratic form of government and human rights are not readily available to great numbers of people in the less developed countries of the world. Texts describe the mechanics of democratic government, speeches praise the ideals, but little is available that focuses on the practical reasons for its necessity. Many people know about democracy and human rights and discuss their implications, but anyone taking part in discussions on these subjects soon has cause to question whether the principles underlying the discussion are fully understood. The wide range of misunderstandings that thus arise, misunderstandings which become more and more accepted as time goes on, creates a serious problem which concerns all thinking men. How does one deal with self-generating misunderstandings of freedom and democracy? How does one put a stop to self-perpetuating distortions of their purposes? Our concern for this problem has impelled us to undertake this volume, to distill the essence of the rationale of freedom and democracy and to put it in language understandable to as many people as can be reached.

In many ways, this has been a difficult and disturbing book to write. Human institutions are not simple; they are not easily cast in terms of necessary and unnecessary, essential and expendable. Democracy and human rights are no exceptions. They mean all things to all men. They have been debased and distorted by embraces from opposite extremes, almost to the point of becoming meaningless. To attempt to identify the critical ingredients that make up a democracy, or to isolate indispensable factors, is indeed a challenging enterprise. One cannot speak of a particular brand of democracy and proclaim that this is equally good for the people in the Cameroons, in British Guiana, in the high Andes, and in a populous European metropolis.

Similarly, the attempt to identify and classify different forms of government necessarily involves oversimplification. An honest look at man, again, does not permit simple answers. The most autocratic regime must respond, in some measure, to the desires of the people; the most democratic must empower certain individuals with authority over their fellow citizens. No comfortable and clear-cut lines are available to enable us to point to one government and say this is a pure democracy, this is a pure oligarchy.

One does not have to ponder these facts long to realize that it is enormously complex, if not impossible, to draw lines of distinction among human institutions. Only the utterly naïve or the charlatan would undertake it with confidence. Nevertheless, one also realizes that the intricacy of human institutions must not be permitted to cause paralysis. There are certain elements that, regardless of whether they are practiced with complete consistency, are rationally identifiable. Even though it may be an oversimplification to insist on these ideals as unique, true, or necessary, our humanity compels us, and our sophistication must not prevent us, from attempting to formulate a concept of what we are seeking. Man may interpret and apply his ideals differently; he may rationalize the need to postpone their consistent adoption in his society. But nevertheless, they do remain as ideals or objectives that society hopes one day to attain.

We have attempted, in this study, to retreat a step from these ideals, to examine not what they are, but why they have become important to us. We discuss the question, not of man's perfect goals, but of what may be the surest way of progressing to a point where we may be able to see those goals more clearly. Given the mortality and the imperfect knowledge of men, we are convinced that the only way to ensure continuing progress toward a better life, with whatever social and economic content one wishes to proclaim as ideal, is to create a system which permits orderly and continuing change in the social and economic structure of the society. Such a system will institutionalize a mechanism to facilitate the expression of the will of the people for such change by providing a meaningful forum for the forces competing in the society, to forge political instruments which can be used to achieve the will of the people.

A continual adjustment of the social and economic life of the society, as man's knowledge and understanding progress, is one of the most important elements of any governmental structure. We are convinced that only democracy provides this mechanism. We have chosen to call it the self-corrective mechanism. It is this self-corrective mechanism which ensures the ultimate progress of man, regardless of social and economic goals, regardless of whether the mechanism operates perfectly or imperfectly. It is the element which ensures the survival, over a long period of time, of a continually progressing society. It is the element that makes democratic institutions so attractive to man in the face of continuing impatience with their apparently slow procedures. That self-corrective mechanism, however, does not function or fulfill men's desires for long without true democratic institutions, which, in turn, depend vitally upon the full exercise of specific human rights.

In explaining principal elements of democracy and of human rights, this book may perhaps seem to be highly utilitarian. It is. This is because democracy is a highly utilitarian system of government. It is dedicated to providing a continuing, responsive system of government in a world which is ridden with opposing beliefs and prejudices. Democracy attempts to do what we have described above as the impossible; it attempts to reconcile the various poles of man's beliefs. It does this, however, not by choosing among them. It does it by embracing man's diversity and by providing a framework in which men may live together. Democracy has little to say about the content of the economic and social theories which many people attempt to link to it. It merely provides the mechanism by which the continuing will of the people may be reflected; accordingly, certain of the competing systems and values may be momentarily accepted.

Although this may sound like the description of a utopia, it is our conviction that such a society is possible. Not only is it possible, but numerous societies are actively struggling to create it and several have made substantial progress.

Finally, before beginning the substance of the study, we wish to express our deep appreciation to and respect for the

members of the Inter-American Commission on Human
Rights, whose discussions and debates have inspired much of
what is contained here. Confronted with enormous problems
shortly after its creation, in 1960, by the Organization of
American States, the Commission has pioneered in the area
of international action on behalf of human rights. Its guidelines were few; its precedents, virtually none. With limited
resources, however, it met the issues with realism and honesty,
attempting to chart a course of meaningful action. The privilege of working with the Commission has illuminated many
of these questions for us, and this volume is, in effect, a summary of the thoughts and ideas evoked as a result of these long
and rewarding discussions.

D. V. S.
L. R. S.

Washington, D.C.
October, 1965

Contents

The FOUNDATIONS *of* FREEDOM

PART ONE

The Problem

A Universal Experience

This study is an attempt to state a relationship between two ideas: human rights and representative democracy. As instruments for man's progress in an intricate, imperfect world, the two have an important practical significance for each other. Because of their interaction, a strict regard for human rights is essential to democracy and, similarly, the democratic principles of self-government are indispensable to ensure the observance of those fundamental rights. Together they comprise a type of self-corrective mechanism which allows for the continuing evolution of mankind's institutions, and constant readjustment to his needs, through orderly and reliable procedures.

The relationship derives from the intrinsic characteristics of the two concepts and cannot be dismissed as solely theoretical. The term human rights refers to the rights of individual man in the context of his relationships with other men in society. As the form of order for the society, government must be appraised in the same framework. That form of government is most desirable which is most effective in fostering these relationships. The two are inevitably linked, due to their common subject.

The connection, however, goes beyond that. One cannot have democracy, within any group, without assuring the members of that group certain rights of which they cannot be deprived arbitrarily. No society can hope to progress if it prevents its principal decision-maker from acquiring all the information necessary to make an informed decision, nor can it expect honest decisions if the decision-maker is fearful of his very existence if he fails to please. And in a self-governing democracy, that decision-maker is every citizen. Nor can one ensure the continuing protection of the rights which enable each citizen to act freely without resting their ultimate control in those who will be affected by their denial. Both elements are part of the same mechanism. They can no more accomplish what they are designed to achieve without each other than a motor is able to drive a machine without a transmission.

The task of defining the interrelationship is not made easier by the manner in which we in the West unquestioningly accept its validity. As elusive as the concepts are when we seek concrete agreement, we have come to accept as axiomatic the premise that man's basic rights are secure only when each man shares equally in the ultimate control over these rights, through his participation in government. It has been called "self-evident"; it is taken for granted as rooted in common sense and the facts of the human personality. This quality of the relationship is revealed, in the Americas, by declarations such as one made by Francisco Bilbao, one of Chile's leading scholars, who stated that "Liberty is political equality, that is to say, democracy properly so-called. This is a . . . fact."[1] What must be accomplished, as far as we in the West are concerned, is to prove an axiom. That is never an easy task. It is not rendered easier by the paradox that great divergencies of opinion arise regarding the implications of these concepts when applied to specific situations.

On the other side of the coin, we confront a world which

sincerely questions the validity of the interrelationship. Our world today is experiencing the strains resulting from the sudden exposure of long-underprivileged groups, through the wonders of mass communication, to the potential economic and social benefits which until now the world has been able to afford only to a comparative few. Moreover, many of the people of today's world have not shared in the great adventure in self-government which is going on in the Western world. Not only do ideas of democracy have a vague meaning to a large segment of humanity, but the desire for immediate material benefits distracts and distorts their significance. The masses of the newly developing nations, the economically deprived, do not care to hear elaborate theories of abstract ideals. What good will rigid observance of human rights and democracy do them in their struggle to gain a better life? This is what they demand to know. In many developing nations, millions of youths are being exposed intensively to the tenets of the Communist philosophy, which holds that civil and political rights are a fiction and expendable in the interest of what that philosophy considers the most important rights of man, the economic rights.

Without deprecating economic rights, it seems necessary to emphasize that, far from being secondary, civil and political rights are the forerunners of economic and social rights; that without civil and political rights to maintain representative government, all men are dependent on the hazardous benevolence of those who are most determined to seize power, no matter what pretensions to social consciousness their government may have. While harsh expedients are sometimes pressed in early stages of economic development to break the grip of a feudalistic power structure, a people that permits its leaders flagrantly or covertly to disregard these principles risks a new feudalism.

For this reason it is essential to illustrate that human rights and democracy, far from being theoretical ideals, are among the most pragmatic and practical notions that man has devised for his own protection and advancement. While one may refer to them as ideals, in the sense that they have nowhere been fully realized in human affairs, the reasons which cause us to insist on them are not theoretical. They are grounded in the facts of man's experience. They are the pragmatic resolution of the problem of what type of social order will be most successful in preventing man from abusing his fellow man. They are the practical instruments to permit mankind to continue experimenting and groping as he seeks a better order for his society. The need for these protections are as real as man himself, and as practical as the tools with which he works the earth. This is not to assert that freedom and the enjoyment of self-government will automatically secure economic and social advancement. It will not. Freedom is only an opportunity. It offers nothing substantive or enduring. Rather, it distributes tremendous responsibilities among all men to take action themselves if good is to be accomplished. As Albert Camus reminded us, freedom is "nothing else but a chance to be better, whereas enslavement is a certainty of the worst."[2] This is the proposition we intend to examine in the body of this study.

A discussion of these concepts must take into account another obstacle: the difficulty of getting man to adhere, consistently, to either of these ideas. The concept of the rights of man, and its corresponding injunction to respect the rights of others, is rooted in man's early history, as an indispensable ingredient of his and other men's survival. William Graham Sumner, the U.S. sociologist, points to its existence in primitive societies.[3] Moses' Ten Commandments set forth rules of conduct which each man has a right to expect from the other. The Bible illustrates its universal elements in the passage reading: "'It is not the manner of the Romans to deliver any man to die, before . . . he which is accused have the accusers face to face, and have license to answer for himself concerning the crime laid against him.'"[4]

From the early experiments in self-government, in Greece and Rome, the concepts of human rights were expanded to include certain political rights which were formulated to enable the government to function efficaciously. About this same time, the belief began to grow that these rights and freedoms could be realized only under self-government. In his *Republic,* Cicero proclaimed that "In no other state save where the power of the people predominates, has liberty any home. Liberty, the sweetest of all blessings, and which if it is not equal for all is not liberty."

Although the beginnings were hesitant and progress slow, the idea was firmly implanted. Regardless of the attempts to uproot liberty, it touched something live, something unquenchable, and could only grow. Hegel even defined history in its terms, as the development of man's consciousness of freedom. Pitted against this increasing consciousness have been the realities of the temptation of power and the innate conservatism of man, a desire to maintain existing institutions intact. A brief scanning of history provides ample confirmation. Time and again a society, in a burst of energy and ideals, will free itself from one set of restrictions and oppressions, only to cling anew to the emerging order, content with a small victory and fearful of proceeding too rapidly to the next challenge. Rome in the time of Caesar, Cromwell's England, Napoleon's France, Latin America in the early nineteenth century, all follow similar patterns. While a few men take advantage of the new conditions to establish their suzerainty, the masses remain inert before the awesome responsibility of power, unconscious of the potential opportunity which is theirs. The former posture of passivity is reassumed while new rules are established and entrench themselves. Patiently, then, men await a new surge to sever the bonds they permit to be re-established. All stages of man's history, all forms of government, appear to repeat the pattern.

Through centuries of incessant struggle, the concepts of human rights and self-government have become increasingly important. Today their inspiration permeates every corner of the earth, every level of society. Distilled from centuries of aspiration and tradition, they are the stake of no single man or nation. As a natural expression of man's long social experience, they have a universality beyond the power of any man or political movement to revise or erase. Thus, while practical application in an imperfect, developing human environment has been difficult, the fact of their universal experience and indomitable growth has been overwhelming. In the belief that men have the capacity to help themselves and in the knowledge that men will not be denied the opportunity to try, freedom and self-government are fundamental to an enduring system of economic and social justice.

The Basic Concepts

A discussion of human rights in their relationship to the form of government known as democracy involves fundamental precepts which we would do well to set forth at the outset. The term "human rights" is employed in two contexts: first, as the broad right of each man to enjoy a happy life, secure from outside interference and, second, as the functional rights which permit a man to act and express himself so that his opinion may be heard and considered in the counsels of the society.

Although no rigid division can be made between the two, certain guidelines can be distinguished. In the first and more universal sense, they comprise those fundamental rights which are rooted in the facts of existence and the dignity of each human being, securing for him the freedom to enjoy his own life as he conceives the meaning and purpose of that life. These rights grant each man the freedom to pursue life in a manner most satisfying to himself—so long as he respects the rights of other men—in his inner or religious life, in choosing the nature of his relationship with his fellow men, in seeking happiness, and indeed, in his basic will to preserve or make his life meaningful. Grounded in the assumption that all men stand on an equal footing of ignorance regarding the ultimate meaning of life, these rights permit each man to seek, as far as he is able, his own sense of purpose. These rights are the announced purpose of all forms of government, and have been expressed in many different ways. The United States Declaration of Independence refers to them as the "unalienable rights" of "Life, Liberty, and the Pursuit of Happiness." They are basic to the design elaborated by John Stuart Mill in his classic treatise *On Liberty:*

> This, then, is the appropriate region of human liberty. It comprises, first, the inward domain of consciousness; demanding liberty of conscience in the most demanding sense; liberty of thought and feeling; absolute freedom of opinion and sentiment on all subjects, practical or speculative, scientific, moral, or theological. The liberty of expressing and publishing opinions . . . being almost of as much importance as the liberty of thought itself, and resting in great part on the same reasons, is practically inseparable from it. Secondly, the principle requires liberty of tastes and pursuits, of framing the plan of our life to suit our own character . . . without impediment from our fellow creatures so long as what we do does not harm them. . . . Thirdly, from this liberty of each individual follows the liberty, within the same limits, of combination among individuals; freedom to unite, for any purpose not involving harm to others. No society in which these liberties are not, on the whole, respected, is free, whatever may be its form of government, and none is completely free in which they do not exist absolute and unqualified.

The second grouping of rights is designed to give practical effect to the first by organizing institutions to ensure those basic freedoms. It is the function of this second group—more commonly known as civil and political rights—to provide a system to order the political activity of the society. Intrinsic in their operation is the recognition that simple declarations by the governing elite that the people are free and that liberty prevails in the country are meaningless unless institutions are incorporated in the organization of the society to guarantee to every citizen that his liberty, as so declared, is secure and that the government is and shall remain responsive to the true wishes of the governed. These rights, sometimes called the political rights, are the means toward achieving the former group of human rights. Human rights, then, in the broad sense, are both the end and the means of man's civil order. They are the end toward which his government must strive and the means by which he can assure that his government does not digress from that purpose. They are fundamentally inseparable.

When we refer to human rights in this study, we will be speaking not of human rights in their broad context, but specifically of those human rights (the civil and political rights) which are essential to the effective operation of a system of government, in this case representative democracy, which will be able effectively to achieve those broader rights. Although the focus of man's vision has broadened to include economic and social rights, and the international declarations formulated in recent years attempt to exhaust all possible expressions and alternatives for the functioning of a democracy, certain political rights remain basic. These political rights are the ones with which we will be concerned.

It is audacious to declare that respect for human rights can only or can best be achieved under a specific form of governmental organization. More than any institutional guarantee, respect for human rights must be inherent in the habits and desires of the people of the society. As the Dutch lawyer and commentator Pieter Drost has observed:

> Cunning political pretenders have time and again succeeded in deceiving the people with predictions and platforms heralding

a social order possessing unique qualities and attributes which are completely separable from the traits and features of the people's character. This dangerous illusion that the state can ever establish a social order which is nobler, worthier, more righteous and more moral than the common citizen, leads to the glorification of the state and to the enslavement of the people.[5]

To this can be added the testimony of Judge Learned Hand that "Liberty lies in the hearts of men and women; when it dies there, no constitution, no law, no court can save it."[6]

No form of government has exclusive claim over recognition of human rights. They can be respected in a monarchy and disregarded in a democracy. The traditions, the maturity, the awareness of the people are as important to their realization as is the form of government. The great Argentine leader of the time of the wars of independence Juan Bautista Alberdi stated the problem in this manner:

If we wish to be free, let us first be worthy of so being. Liberty does not come all of a sudden. It is a slow part of civilization. It is not the conquest of a day; it is one of humanity's ends, an end which we shall never achieve wholly. . . . The people that will be free must be industrious, artistic, philosophical, believing, moral. Let one of these elements be lacking and we return to barbarism.[7]

Nonetheless, the experience of man, as reinforced by repeated expressions of his most thoughtful representatives, affirms that certain elements in a government ensure that those broader goals are best achieved under the form of government known as representative democracy. As long ago as ancient Greece and Rome, philosophers emphatically asserted that no man could be considered free unless he participated in the political processes.[8] When the rights of man were first embodied in official public documents in 1776 and 1789, it was assumed without question that democracy was the most efficacious means for attaining those rights, even though that democracy was far from representative of all men. One of the principal elements in that rationale, in addition to the axiom that freedom meant self-government, was that the dispersion of the base of power prevented its usurpation and distortion, and consequently served to maintain those rights intact for longer periods. This was expressed by Thomas Jefferson when he affirmed that "there is no safe depository of the ultimate powers of society but the people themselves."

The intense spirit of human rights and democracy which pervaded that era was intrinsically linked to the new spirit of humanism, which, in many respects, clung to the historical threads of natural rights. As such, they were relegated to a sphere beyond human doubt, and stood even above constitutions as innerent and inalienable for all men. As these rights were conceived, they were not created by the state, nor could they be rescinded by the state. Indeed, a right to revolution was invoked in their name; the United States Declaration of Independence proclaimed that "whenever any Form of Government becomes destructive of these ends, it is the Right of the People to alter or to abolish it." Throughout this revolutionary epoch, human rights, humanism, and individualism were all summoned to limit the powers of government, whose function was deemed to be solely to arbitrate and adjudicate conflicting interests. Human rights were considered safe so long as the state had no control over them. From this thought came the stark, absolute terms of the Bill of Rights of the United States.

Today, with the eighteenth-century ideals of limited government generally regarded as untenable, the concepts of fundamental political rights are also under strong attack by those who proclaim that economic and social rights are the foundation of man's civic order. Man himself appears to be trying to decree that man has no foreordained rights, that there is nothing about man's nature which cannot be changed, that man's rights are subject to the will of man.

With the incessant and irresistible demands for social and economic justice occupying the concern of humanity, man's rights are everywhere being subordinated to these demands. From the upsurge of awareness of economic and social rights has come a tendency to play down the historic antagonism between human freedom and government authority. Rather than fearing an inevitably more powerful and potentially all-encompassing government, the advocates of these rights rely upon the active support of government and organized society to attain them. Far from eclipsing the concept of civil and political rights, however, the broad and ever-expanding sphere of government action has given them a new urgency. The great issue of our time has become the need to ensure that government, increasingly powerful and potentially irre-sistible, remains fully responsive to the needs of the people and does not fall under the control of those who set themselves up as the sole interpreters of man's needs.

This is increasingly difficult because Communism, the other pole of the conflicting forces in today's world, maintains that, regardless of the wishes of individual man, the state must proceed to mold a new world based on the premise that the interest of the community of men is paramount to the rights and interest of individual man. In so doing, however, there is an element of contradiction. In denying the justice of civil and political rights, they seem to be affirming that some other concept of justice exists beyond the influence of the presently expressed desires of individual men. By this concept, they claim to measure the utility of existing human institutions and to guide those who will wield the power of government in the future they will build. Although the mystical force of this greater justice sanctions the destruction of mankind's existing institutions, they rarely explain how, in seeking to achieve their conception of the greater economic rights, they will avoid the great pitfall of history, the abuse of power. How shall government, composed of fallible men, be spared these abuses which they assert have permeated the other forms of economic and social power in man's history? The fact is, there is no way to avoid abuse; no foolproof method exists to prevent men and governments from abusing their powers. The best man is able to do is to create institutions which will afford adequate and impartial procedures and remedies to the citizens to redress violations and abuses when they occur. No government which does not contain such institutions can long ensure respect for any of the rights of its people.

Adolf Berle recently pointed out the implications of the new awareness of the importance of social and economic justice, especially for Latin America:

Intellectuals in many of these countries . . . surveying the contrast between great wealth and abject poverty . . . make a charge. If, they say, this is what Christian civilization produces . . . it has failed. The real task is to construct a new civilization on a new theory and a new base. Not infrequently such comments are a prelude to an argument in favor of Communist revolution, although not because of any conversion to Marxism or any liking for the tyranny that exists in Communist states. They reflect a passionate desire to escape, somehow, from the nineteenth-century organization of affairs out of which current Latin American life seems to provide no exit save by revolution.

North Americans do not readily understand this. We ourselves have never adequately formulated the theory and method of the social-economic system prevailing in the United States. In its own empiric fashion, the United States has developed a system which relegates Marxian communism to the museum of nineteenth-century thought. That is, we have at one and the same time achieved a vast increase of production, a vast increase of distribution, and an enduring system of individual liberty. We have done this peacefully. This made it possible for the United States to abolish the proletariat rather than enthrone it. The United States had a long head start resulting from a century and a half of compulsory, free, common education—a condition which does not exist in most of Latin America today—and the fruits of a great deal of experimentation in the various state and local governments. But we have never explained those processes in readily understandable theory.[9]

Because of the critical importance of the processes of which Mr. Berle speaks for the economic and social advancement of mankind, it is important that an attempt be made to explain them. Although we have not undertaken in this study a detailed examination of the role of economic and social rights, certainly we do not underestimate their importance. Today, it is indisputably acknowledged that the need for higher living standards, eradication of poverty and ignorance, protection from unemployment, and a progressive improvement in cultural, hygienic, and sanitary conditions are fundamental to preclude "living conditions so intolerable that no government could be worse."[10] It is equally true, however, that such economic and social progress is integrally related to, and implicit in, liberty under democratic government. This was stressed by the UNESCO Advisory Committee on Human Rights in stating that liberty means:

the positive organization of the social and economic conditions within which men can participate to a maximum as active members of the community and contribute to the welfare of the community at the highest level permitted by the material development of the society. This liberty can have meaning only under democratic conditions, for only in democracy is liberty set in that context of equality which makes it an opportunity for all men and not for some men only.[11]

Clearly, it is becoming ever more urgent today to examine the ideas of democracy, and especially the concepts of human rights, from the pragmatic viewpoint of their relationship to the purpose and form of government and the great economic goals we have set before ourselves. First of all, it must be observed that democracy, as a political system, has little to say about the substantive content of the economic or social theories which prevail. It is a process which can thrive as well in the socialist atmosphere of Sweden as in the extreme individualistic societies in their formative years. Within it, human rights are not an idealistic aspiration. They have a practical function: they serve to place the institutions man has devised for his more effective government, whatever they may be, beyond the vicissitudes of political extremes, beyond the whim of those who temporarily hold power—even though they be majorities—and establish them as firm institutions which cannot be transgressed because of expediency.

Without deprecating economic rights, it is a fact that civil and political rights are the forebears of economic and social rights; that without civil and political rights to establish true representative government, all men are dependent on the capricious benevolence of those who happen to seize power, no matter how socially conscious their government pretends to be. Civil and political rights are essential to the cause of individual freedom, without which democracy could not flourish. Most important, they establish the design of a system of government which contains within itself a self-corrective mechanism, by which man's rebellion against what he feels to be unjust in his environment can be expressed and adjusted in an orderly process. This, then, is the fundamental aim of democracy: to provide the mechanism for orderly change and continual accommodation to man's emerging needs.

Alexander Meiklejohn has described the mechanism in this way:

> Our plan of government, being based on imperfect knowledge, must be forever open to amendment, forever on trial. It will change as social conditions change, and as human insight changes. And no one can tell in advance how slow or how quick, how superficial or how radical, those changes will be. We, the People, acting under the Constitution, will decide, from time to time, on that issue. And our successors will be

free, as we are, to determine what form, for them, the government shall take.[12]

Our generation has embarked on an ambitious plan to secure all human rights—economic, social, and political—to all men. These rights must be secured; they do not automatically exist. To secure them, some mechanism is needed and that mechanism is government. Only in the knowledge that the fundamental civil and political rights are respected by their government, however, can the people be certain that their government does not digress from its avowed purpose of securing the greater welfare of all the people. The day-to-day functioning and practices of that government leave a deep imprint on the rights which they seek to attain. It is the conviction of Western civilization that representative democracy is the most honest, enduring, and efficacious method of government to attain these ends.

Defining Representative Democracy and Human Rights

Aware of the extreme reactions aroused in men by the most common of ideas, one is not surprised to find few able to agree on a definition of "democracy" and "human rights." We are all for them, but *what* are we for? The words have been accorded as many different meanings as there are systems of values in the world. Most important for our purposes, however, are the different meanings which the two great opposing ideologies in the world today place on the words, each proclaiming that its purpose is to achieve a true democracy. In our hemisphere, this confusion of words has been dramatized by the events in Fidel Castro's Cuba, where the revolution embarked with the proclamation of embracing "the purest principles of representative democracy, fully recognizing the basic human freedoms, with an absolute respect for human rights as set forth in the Charter of Bogotá and in inter-American and world conventions."[13]

A hundred years ago, Abraham Lincoln tried to pinpoint the dilemma presented by the use of the word "liberty":

> The world has never had a good definition of the word liberty, and the American people, just now, are much in want of one. We all declare for liberty; but in using the same *word* we do not all mean the same *thing*. With some the word liberty may mean for each man to do as he pleases with himself, and the product of his labor; while with others, the same word may mean for some men to do as they please with other men, and the product of other men's labor. Here are two, not only different, but incompatible things called by the same name— liberty. And it follows that each of the things is, by the respective parties, called by two different and incompatible names— liberty and tyranny.[14]

The several connotations of these words make it important that we set forth their meaning as we shall use them here, which is basically in the original and most fundamental sense. According to its Greek origins, *demos* (the people) and *kratos* (authority), "democracy" means that the ultimate authority is vested in the people, or in the words of Montesquieu, "when the body of the people is possessed of the supreme power."[15] In the United States Declaration of Independence, it is expressed as government by the consent of the governed. Whatever other meanings or implications may attach, therefore, the essential criterion of democracy is that it places primary importance on, and attempts to reflect, the will of the people composing the society. In speaking of representative democracy, we are referring to a method by which the authority of the people is exercised indirectly through representatives.

Questions quickly arise: Who are the people? How do we know when that authority is invoked? How do we know when their consent is expressed? In the early democracies, "the people" were a small percentage of the population. In the United States, in the first presidential election, when George Washington ran unopposed, only 5 per cent of the population voted.[16] But the composition of "the people" has consistently expanded. Today, even in the developing countries which profess a theory of democracy through one-party rule, it is acknowledged that "the people" are a majority of the total population of the society. Although all countries draw lines of eligibility, such as the common one of nationality, virtually all men born or pledging allegiance to that society are recognized as components of the amorphous mass known as "the people."

A more complex question arises when we ask how we know when the consent of the people is expressed. Where a "one-party" democracy exists, or when the means by which the people participate in selecting and nominating the candidates for election are limited, with the consequent narrowing of their ultimate choice, how can we honestly determine the true will of the people? This question has long disturbed analysts and advocates of democracy. In truth, there is no foolproof method of achieving or knowing this. The most elemental means, however, and the closest man has approached to direct consultation of the people for the purpose of constructing a fully self-governing society, is through the process of elections. The American Declaration of Rights and Duties of Man, adopted in 1948 by the American republics at the Ninth International Conference of American States in Bogotá, states that participation in government is the right of all men, and defines such participation in these terms:

> Article XX. Every person having legal capacity is entitled to participate in the government of his country, directly or through his representatives, and to take part in popular elections, which shall be by secret ballot, and shall be honest, periodic and free.

Thus, implicit in the choosing of a representative are elections, which are defined as being by secret ballot, at specific intervals, under conditions of honesty that ensure the free and true expression of the people's will. These elections, with these safeguards, are the mechanism which places the ultimate veto power in the hands of the citizens of the state. It is the most effective instrument that has been devised to ensure that government is and remains representative and expressive of the people's wishes. When we refer to democracy in this study, therefore, the concept of elections will be an implicit assumption.

The essential rationale of this method of government is that absolute authority shall not be vested in any one man or group of men to determine the needs and desires of other men, or to dictate or judge what is good or bad, proper or improper for the society, contrary to the wishes of the men who compose that society. Such a rationale demands a system whereby all men who serve the state, in or out of public office, can be held to account to the people. In this respect, it differs fundamentally from Communism and the so-called "people's democracies," in which the criterion of the democracy is not whether there are elections or other safeguards to ascertain the true will of the people, but whether the person holding power claims to represent a specific class. When that power is in the hands of those who come from, and claim to represent, exclusively the workers, or proletariat, then the democracy is considered to be authentic.

In truth, there is at present little communication or understanding between these opposing theories. The Western democracies are repelled by the presumptuousness of the Communist parties in arrogating to themselves the authority for interpreting the will of the people. The historical experience of mankind vividly illustrates how the forcible repression of dissenting groups is incompatible with any concept of a free society. In the eloquent words of Albert Camus: "there is no possible evolution in a totalitarian society. Terror does not evolve except toward worse terror, the scaffold does not become any more liberal, the gallows are not more tolerant.

Nowhere in the world has there been a party or a man with absolute power who did not use it absolutely."[17]

The Communists, for their part, ridicule what they consider to be the feeble pretense of a number of Western nations to cloak oligarchies of money and property in the respectable dress of democracy. This completely misses the point. Oligarchies are not democracies. A society that effectively shuts out large elements of its population, by refusing to educate them to the responsibilities of self-government, is not reflecting the wishes of those groups so deprived. The larger that segment is, the smaller becomes the definition of "the people" whose consent is sought, until, at the extreme, it can become hardly distinguishable from a dictatorship. Whatever self-justifications are invoked for oligarchical systems of government, they do not come within the definition of democracy, for under a true democracy the wielders of money and power can be maintained only when they are effective in providing a good life or otherwise satisfying the balance of the society, while permitting them free expression. As with every other system of government, including those espoused by its critics, the ideal form of democracy has not been attained. The urgent question for this generation is how to transform existing oligarchies into democratic structures without undergoing the destruction and suffering that attend total revolution.

The fundamental principles of the democratic system, underlying the mechanisms which are necessary to its effective functioning, reflect this purpose to give expression to the total society. Although it is not our intention to enter into an analysis of the administrative operations of government, three principles of the mechanism of democracy are important to an understanding of its significance. These principles must be observed by those entrusted with public power, or the democracy will be transformed rapidly into something quite different: (1) to establish the supremacy of the laws over the individual will of men; (2) to incorporate in the system a process of altering the law according to the true will of the people; and (3) to establish full protection so that no small portion of the society may distort the authority of the law to their own devices.

The importance of the supremacy of the laws in a democracy is rooted in John Locke's premise that "wherever law ends, tyranny begins." All men holding the reins of public power must be bound by pre-established norms of conduct and law in all decisions affecting their fellow citizens. Moreover, that law must be beyond individual manipulation. The supreme law, by which all public servants are bound, and on which the citizens may rely regardless of who exercises temporal power or who comprises the majority at any given time, is the constitution of the state. That constitution invariably contains severe restrictions on the power of the state to invade those rights which are considered essential to the proper functioning of the democracy, and their embodiment in that document emphasizes that they may not be abrogated or rewritten without the express consent of the people.

Second, to protect the society from rigid laws, and to ensure the adaptability of the system to a changing world, there must be a process of altering those laws by peaceful procedures acceptable to the persons composing the society. The manner in which this is done must reflect the basic philosophy of the democratic system: the purpose of the state is to serve the interests of its citizens and to meet the changing needs and desires of those citizens. This is effected through direct and indirect consultation with the people via elections; it is the people themselves who proclaim their decision through their right to vote and their right to make the laws through their chosen representatives. As we stated earlier, these elections are implicit in the system of representative democracy and indeed are the *sine qua non* of such government. Montesquieu affirmed that:

In a democracy the people are in some respects the sovereign, and in others, the subject. There can be no exercise of sovereignty except by their suffrage which are their own wills. . . . The laws therefore, which establish the right of suffrage, are fundamental to the government.[18]

Through that right of suffrage, the people are able, in an orderly process, to exercise their will to change the law when it becomes inadequate to their needs, and thus they can ensure the adaptability and adequacy of the government to their needs. Although they retain the ultimate control of the government of the democracy, the people do not make the practical day-to-day decisions. Their control is exercised through the selection of their representatives and their leaders, through the ultimate power of veto on those representatives who do not comply with their wishes. While they cannot participate in every decision, they are the final arbiters on whether those holding public trust are acting in disregard of or in the interest of the society. It is an indirect control over policy, exercised through direct control over the policy-makers. It is in the selection of their leaders, and the manner in which that leadership must operate, that democracy distinguishes itself from other forms of government which may, indeed often do, adopt similar public policies. The most significant result of this process is the operation of a self-corrective mechanism by which the people are able to make errors, change their minds, and correct their errors. It is this mechanism which establishes the vitality and durability of the democratic method. Regardless of what economic and social theories prevail, the way remains open to correct the errors and the false directions a society may take.

Third, to guarantee the existence of a true democracy, there must be established a method of protection so that no group may arrogate to itself the power of the state. To attain this end, representative democracy incorporates the principle of separation of powers. By this concept, which was essential in Montesquieu's early scheme, the separate powers of the legislature, executive, and judiciary are able to check and prevent abuses which may be perpetrated by one of the other branches of government. Whereas in practice these may overlap, and critics may point out the usurpation of power by one branch over another, in practice the existence of these checks operates to allow the people to protect their own interests more satisfactorily than any alternatives which man has devised. Agustín Alvarez, the Argentine scholar, affirmed these principles when he emphasized that words alone would never ensure a respect for the rights of people; only an effective system of checks and balances between the coordinate powers of government could ensure this.[19]

The term "rights," and its cognate ideas, justice and liberty, are more difficult to define, for, as we have already mentioned, its definition depends greatly on the underlying system of values. In a strict legal sense, a "right" is defined as "that which a person is entitled to have, to do, or to receive from others, within the limits prescribed by law."[20] In reference to a democracy, these rights often have a largely negative sense, and similar in tone to the Ten Commandments' "Thou shalt not," the directives are pointed at the government with the equivalent of "Congress shall make no law." They set forth that sphere of activity upon which the government may not encroach and outline those prerogatives of the people which must remain inviolate in order to provide the basis for the free development of human institutions. Even Hegel, one of the classic exponents of the dominant role of the state, acknowledged the indispensable role of rights in the formulation of the activities of the state. He declared in his *Philosophy of Right:*

> The essence of the modern state is that the universal be bound up with the complete freedom of its particular members and with private well-being, that thus the interests of the family

and civil society must concentrate themselves on the state, although the universal end cannot be advanced without the personal knowledge and will of its particular member, *whose own rights must be maintained* [italics added].[21]

Although Hegel casts his concept of individual rights in an entirely different context, it is instructive that he considers that those rights cannot be overlooked by any system. Respect for them is elemental to all systems. In a democracy, they refer to a protection for the individual against the superior force of government, which is expressed in a number of the constitutions of the several states of the United States of America in the phrase, "absolute and arbitrary power over the lives, liberty and property of free men exists nowhere in a republic, not even in the largest majority."[22]

These rights also connote positive ideas. Each one serves a definite, essential, and practical function. This sense of the meaning of the concept "rights" will be considered as we seek to enumerate and define the significance of each individual right.

The Relationship Between Democracy and Human Rights

The intimate relationship between the respect for human rights and the practice of democracy is readily observed in the natural association these ideas have in men's minds. As was pointed out earlier, we often tend to accept that relationship as axiomatic. However, in an age where the vast majority of mankind is alien to the benefits which this form of government is able to provide, this is a perilous assumption to make. Not only lack of experience with these ideas, but the goals which the society establishes for itself, affect its concept of that relationship. As Hans Kelsen has declared:

Democracy is a just form of government only because it is a form of government by which individual freedom is preserved.

That means that it is a just form of government under the condition that individual freedom is presupposed as an ultimate end. If, instead of individual freedom, social security is presupposed and if it can be proved that social security cannot be established under a democratic form of government, then not democracy, but another form of government may be considered as just, since another end requires another means. Hence democracy can be justified only as a relatively—not as an absolutely—just form of government.[23]

Even Kelsen, however, makes the basic assumption that "democracy is just . . . because . . . individual freedom is preserved." The question, however, is: What is the relationship between individual freedom and democracy? Is it essential? How does one contribute to the other? Can one exist without the other? The "if" that Kelsen poses regarding the attainment of other social values under other forms of government is an important one. Perhaps other social values and economic goals, if they are to endure, are also uniquely related to these ideas. Perhaps the relationship between democracy and human rights is so vital, so fundamental to the conduct of human affairs, that it affects all aspects of our cultural and personal development.

It is difficult to take an unbiased view of these questions. The relationship did not become axiomatic to much of the world without good cause. But the identity of the relationship in men's minds is more than a wish for a better life; there is a practical, pragmatic interaction which is vastly important for all areas of human conduct. Together they create a system which allows for man's fallibility and weakness, yet does not permit those elements to become irreparably predominant. Together they create a self-corrective mechanism which permits all manner of social experiment and yet provides for the continuing accommodation of mankind's emerging needs. To recast an old saying, they institutionalize change so that they may remain the same.

These elements of the relationship of human rights and democracy come into focus if we pose some basic questions: In what way does the observance of and respect for the rights of the individual human being contribute to the most effective conduct of the affairs of man and the advancement of the community? This raises the question as to what we expect the order of the community—its government—to attain. By our definition of what government is designed to achieve, we can distinguish what rights might best contribute to its functioning. But what we want government to attain derives from what we consider to be the nature and necessities of man, from which the rights of man are derived, and which government must respect if it is to be effective. It is the proverbial vicious circle which links together one's belief in democracy with a specific concept of man's rights, and vice versa. We do, however, reach one point where we can grasp something fundamental. That is *knowledge*. Knowledge among men is a rare commodity. To what extent can any one man know all of men's needs? All men are mortal; no man is omniscient. History indisputably dramatizes the differing views of different epochs concerning what those needs are. No durable system can be constructed unless it recognizes the basic facts of mortality and fallibility. Although absolute knowledge and absolute values are cherished by man, the stark fact is that men violently disagree concerning what those absolutes are. Who is right? Who determines who is right? Albert Camus underscored man's dilemma in this area: "What [he] wants is to defend absolute values, such as modesty and man's divine truth, when the things that should be defended are the few provisional values that will allow [him] to continue fighting, someday, and comfortably, for those absolute values."[24]

This one sentence contains the essence of democracy and human rights. It also reveals the core of the problem of humanity. We all have our own notions of what is right—and we never cease challenging each other's ideas. But if any one of these ideas gained predominance and sought to repress all other competing concepts, life would become intolerable. The only really important idea is to create the environment whereby we can all continue groping and exploring for what may someday lead to a clearer view of what may be truth.

Regardless of what changes are desired, the mechanism for change must be established and maintained. The way must remain open for all men—wise men and apparent fools—to record their opinions fearlessly so that man can seek truth, as it concerns him, where he will. The way must remain open for all men—wise men and fools—to record their opinion fearlessly about the proper ordering of man's relations with the society of man.

Thus the principal link between human rights and democracy derives from what one considers to be the situation of man and the aim of his government. In truth, man is continually striving to acquire knowledge and to improve the conditions of his life. The human situation will allow no one man or group of men to claim a monopoly of knowledge, and on the basis of that knowledge claim a monopoly of power. Abuse is inevitable. Unfettered participation of the people in the control of their institutions is the only enduring method of providing for and ensuring fairness and just application to the needs of all. In this sense, both human rights and democracy gain much through association. They allow for imperfection, on the part of both the rulers and the ruled. They allow for errors to be made, and for errors to be corrected, without completely upsetting the basic structure of the society.

In history, human rights and democracy are frequently found so intimately related that they are, in fact, defined through association. As conceived in the *Declaration of the Rights of Man and Citizen* of the French Revolution, "the aim of every political association is the preservation of the natural and imprescriptible rights of man," and "the source of all sovereignty is essentially in the nation; nobody, no individual can exercise authority that does not proceed from it in plain terms."[25] The relationship is that representative democracy offers the clearest and most positive consensus of the sentiment of man concerning his vital interests, and is the most accurate means yet devised for providing positive guidance for the sovereign power which is the nation. If the people seek improvement or change in quest of the full realization of their capacities as human beings and a greater measure of individual liberty, their will can be most effectively expressed in an operating system of democratic government.

Most important, human rights are a necessary counterweight to the otherwise overwhelming power of the state and highly organized interests and professionally guided pressure groups seeking to influence the state. Camus realized this when he sought to enjoin those who considered their ideas to be the truest from imposing their "true ideas" on others, should they acquire power. In a passionate plea for the protection of the individual against the potential all-consuming state, he warned:

> Those who cause the most blood to flow are the same ones who believe they have right, logic and history on their side. Hence our society must now defend herself not so much against the individual as against the State. It may be that the proportions will be reversed in another thirty years. But, for the moment, our self-defense must be aimed at the State first and foremost. Justice and expediency command the law to protect the individual against a State given over to the follies of sectarianism or of pride. . . . Forbidding a man's execution would amount to proclaiming publicly that society and the State are not absolute values, that nothing authorizes them to legislate definitely or to bring about the irreparable.[26]

Even were we not convinced, the law of probability should make us think twice. Given the reality of man's capacity and will, it is far more probable that the vast concentration of power in the hands of the modern state may be abused to the detriment of the people, than it is probable that any individual citizen, no matter how powerful he may be, could endanger the existence of the state.

The abuse of power by those who would control the state is, indeed, the principal danger against which the citizens of a society must guard. Man is imperfect; transgressions of trust are easy and always tempting. In 1960, a report of the Inter-American Peace Committee, seeking to determine the relationship of violations of human rights to the maintenance of peace, stated:

> The peoples of this continent know that absolute power, whatever form it may take or under whatever pretext it is seized, soon ends in moral and political as well as material corruption. Therefore they increasingly perceive the truth . . . that . . . the solidarity of the American States require their political organization on the basis of the effective exercise of representative democracy which, in turn, must rest upon a guarantee of the rights of man.[27]

The Declaration of the Rights of Man and Citizen, in its preamble, characterized the problem in the following terms: "ignorance, neglect, or contempt of the rights of man are the sole causes of the public miseries and of the corruption of governments." The solution to the ever-present danger of the abuse of power is to disperse political power over a broad base and, to ensure the continuation of that distribution of power, to give each man a stake in its preservation. That stake is *freedom.* But only in combination with democracy does the freedom of the individual have an opportunity to operate, within an institutionalized system, to call to account those who hold public power, thereby serving to minimize abuse of power and its degenerating influences. Even then, the perils are far from dissipated.

The relationship must be considered in the context of the modern world: the speed of communications; the tremendous concentrations of economic power in the hands of industry, labor, and government; the impatience for rapid advancement; the well-developed psychological techniques at the disposal of unscrupulous people who seek to exploit them for their own ends. One of the principal crises for democracy today arises when those who gain power, through legitimate or quasi-legitimate democratic procedures, betray the trust which comes into their hands and, paying only verbal homage to democratic forms and guarantees, invoke the techniques of modern propaganda and the overt threats of state power to stifle the opposition. In the Western Hemisphere today, the Alliance for Progress has been launched in recognition of the fact that, in many countries, the democratic institutions provided for in written constitutions have failed to loosen the grip of a small oligarchy on the economic and political life of these nations, leaving the framework of democracy devoid of substance.

What responses can be made to a people under the control of a demagogue who employs the forms of democracy to deny real democracy? How can one institute or re-create a democracy when no democratic methods are permitted in the society, and human rights are a fiction? What happens when the mass of people are denied economic and social benefits or opportunities, while those who hold power claim that power in the name of free elections under a democracy? Where are the "self-corrective mechanisms" then? Where does one turn for change? Do we say to them, "Wait," while in some mystical way we go about perfecting democracy?

The alternatives often posed are force and violent revolution, in contrast to the idea of working gradually, through fortifying the economy, expanding education, improving the awareness of the people, and thus aiding the society to evolve toward a democracy. Fidel Castro appeals to the people of the Americas to embrace the former solution; the latter course, charted by the Alliance for Progress, sometimes appears tedious and uncertain, and cynics glibly scoff at its idealistic note. But the facts of history are on its side. Wherever the will of the people has sought expression by means of force, the people have generally lost control to a new elite, who assumed the oppressing role of the old, and the benefits which the masses sought continued to be denied to them. Equally important is a vision of the type of society which is likely to emerge from the differing techniques. If one group is disposed to act by force and violence, it is establishing a precedent for those who are being deposed to re-establish their ascendancy by similar means. To insist on immediate and violent correction of the errors of the past, the errors of our fathers and the generations of mankind before them, is to sanction an interminable conflict and creation of a society whose only order will be that of superior force.

The approach of democracy may not seem appealing to those who seek immediate results, but no firm evidence has ever been adduced that a better life will certainly be achieved more rapidly under other methods, which involve much greater risks. It is hoped that a fuller understanding of the relationship between an authentic respect for human rights and democracy may aid us in making these decisions.

Finally, the relationship between human rights and democracy exists because democracy cannot function without a certain respect for those rights. If democracy relies on the expression of the will of the people, that will can be verified only when conditions exist for (1) the formulation of that will based on full information concerning the conduct of the people's affairs, (2) the expression of that will by means of speech and elections, and (3) the check on elected officials by means of public opinion, publicity, and elections. In turn, this implies freedom from the fear of the destruction or injuring of life or well-being, if that will is honestly expressed, and remedies if any threats are posed to the exercise of these rights. This entire mechanism of safeguards and self-correction is the essence of the orientation of the civil and political rights of democratic government.

Theory Versus Practice

Many countries have elaborate constitutional guarantees for the basic human rights and liberties examined in this study. In the Western Hemisphere, every single nation has such provisions.[28] The experience of history, however, impressively demonstrates that the validity of those guarantees extends only as far as those who control the mechanism of government permit. Here in the Western Hemisphere, several countries— Chile, Brazil, Mexico, Costa Rica, and Uruguay, to name a few—have an excellent record of respecting these human rights, and a diligent system of judicial protection; in most others, however, at one point or another in their recent history, the practice belies the ideal. This can occur in either of two ways: by legal measures in outright derogation of those rights (we shall examine such measures in Part Three, when we discuss permissible limitations on these rights), or else by formal adherence to the theoretical principles accompanied by the imposition of barriers to their practical realization.

The world is not unfamiliar with the masquerade of a strict, almost punctilious regard for all human rights on paper when, in practice, none exist. The leaders of the state can assert that they permit full freedom of expression. The use of that freedom to question the policies of the government, however, will deprive the speaker of other rights, or cause him to be imprisoned on trumped-up charges. He may even disappear if he takes his freedoms too seriously. Should a third party petition to inquire about the person who has disappeared, the police, and even the President may send proper replies; the party will be requested to fill out every imaginable form and file papers, and will receive meticulous, detailed replies to each. Every "protection" can be afforded; but the one who disappeared will never be found. When this occurs with sufficient frequency, the citizens learn what is expected of them. Jesús de Galíndez, in his excellent exposé of the Trujillo dictatorship in the Dominican Republic (the validity of which was supported by his own unexplained disappearance) observed that "again we are confronted with an apparent freedom of political . . . association. . . . On paper, the Dominican legislation is one of the most liberal."[29] Such happenings are not atypical. Human rights are frequently repressed without altering the verbal homage that is accorded them or the concept of democracy. It is this practice that has traditionally posed the greatest threat to human rights.

The problem is not one limited to our times. It was inherited from the first tentative steps mankind took toward these ideals, and in a sense is implicit in the very idea of evolution toward a better world. But if the inconsistencies were evident in the formative stages of all the great democracies of the world, the contrast was most striking in the Latin American republics. Their independence was merely a change of personnel from a European monarchy to a new type of authoritarian control by the local elite. Although the wars of independence were waged in Latin America in terms of the French Declaration of the Rights of Man and Citizen, and the U.S. Declaration of Independence, these were largely implements in a struggle against a foreign king; strong political forces pressed for establishing a local monarchy or life-long presidents. As Ciro Alegría of Peru explains, "nearly everyone wanted government by force."[30] Bolívar was made lifelong President of Peru; Sucre assumed a similar role in Bolivia; Brazil retained her monarch almost until the twentieth century. Democracy was the sound of the words on people's lips; the practices were far different. This dichotomy between words and practices has continued into modern times.

As anomalous as it may seem, there is an element of hope arising from these contradictions. This has been nowhere

better expressed than by former Governor Luis Muñoz Marín
of Puerto Rico:

> I know that . . . in a hemisphere dedicated to democracy . . .
> democracy does not approach perfection in the same degree
> everywhere. What makes our hemisphere the hemisphere of
> democracy is not the more or less complete realization of de-
> mocracy in its different regions: it is its evident purpose of
> democracy, its persistent dream of democracy. There have been
> dictatorships in the American hemisphere, but there has never
> been a dictator that has dared to withhold the respect that
> must be rendered to democratic principles in America. No one
> in the American hemisphere has dared to justify a dictatorship
> with a philosophy holding that dictatorship is good. No one in
> the American hemisphere has dared, as the fascist dictators
> have dared, to proclaim that they govern in the capacity of men
> to be slaves, that they govern in the name of the incapacity of
> men to be free. That reality shown in the universal respect to
> the principle of democracy in the whole of America is what
> makes America the hemisphere of democracy.

When viewed through the perspective of history, the skepti-
cism gives way to cautious hope. Ingrained social mores and
customs are not easily transformed; a disposition and tolerance toward gradual change, however, can be built into our
habits. Where this is done, the pace of change increases as
time passes. Even though not practiced with consistency, the
ideals which a society professes, or to which it pays lip service,
have a way of taking concrete form without anyone quite being aware of how it occurred. Henri Bergson describes this
process as it has taken place in primitive societies and modern
civilizations.[31] The seemingly endless circle in which a society
revolves, as it professes certain ideals but ignores them in
practice, as it goes about accommodating itself to the necessities and the insecurities of life, is not really inescapable. The
ideals inject an unaccountable and uncontrollable element
which ferments with the generations, and, like a centrifugal

force, as the society goes around that circle, pushes it more and more to a point where it spills over and is released from the confines which once held it. Ideals, repeated often enough, do become realities. This is the promise of democracy.

As an example, no one maintains that the United States, from its formative years, consistently adhered to the ideals of freedom and untrammeled human rights for all men. Slavery existed for seventy-five years in spite of our Bill of Rights; political equality was denied to women until 1920; in World War I, more than 2,000 persons were imprisoned for speech and publications, and in World War II, entire racial minorities were uprooted and moved to segregated areas. In the process, however, certain ideals which were imbedded in the theory of the society were percolating more and more to the surface. A clear illustration of the transformations that can occur may be observed in the "accommodation" with segregation made for many years by the United States. Gradually, it gives way as the ideals which the society professes push it further and further toward an honest confrontation with itself. Even though it appeared for many decades that the country would never emerge successfully from the vicious and seemingly inescapable circle in which it had caught itself, the gradual diffusion of and belief in the ideal of human dignity, preserved through orderly institutions, was irrepressible. So it may well be with human rights and democracy in the world today. Ideals have meaning. They set the standard by which we judge our own and our fellow citizen's action. When the day arrives that the men who believe in them outnumber and outvote those who seek to repress them, changes begin. And when that moment arrives, they occur in a manner in keeping with the ideals which are sought.

Throughout this process a certain momentum must be maintained, so that the gap between the theory and the practice of respect for human rights and the exercise of democracy does not become self-destructive. If, after an ideal saturates a society, those who retain power continue to repress the true expression of the people of that society, men lose hope. When hope fades, and ideals appear patently hypocritical, the mysterious promise of other untried ideals becomes attractive. Today, in many areas of the world, democracy is faced with this dilemma. Its name has been invoked so often by those who abuse it that it is becoming distorted and discredited. Time is no longer expendable. In the interest of the freedom and well-being of all men, our institutions must sincerely seek to benefit all men. Those who today use the words of freedom as a camouflage for repression are effectively helping to sow the seeds of repression of freedom, and especially their own freedom.

In the great struggle engaging mankind today, more is at stake than the material goal of economic development. The principal issue is that of man and the state. Those forces extolling economic rights as of primary importance, proclaiming their supremacy over political rights, ground their argument in Hegel's thesis that the state is the supreme end, and subject only to its own will. They interpret jurisprudence and political rights as the will of the ruling group imposed on the society as a law for all.[32] They rationalize that only a powerful, single-minded government is capable of undertaking the long-range planning and operations needed for the economic development of society. All views contrary to that of the state are to be suppressed; as Andrei Vishinsky put it, "there can be no place for freedom of speech, press, and so forth for the foes of socialism."[33] Another Soviet theoretician was thus able to declare:

> What seems high treason to democracy leaves Soviet citizens unmoved, as they are citizens of a classless society, and, therefore without conflicting interests. In the U.S.S.R. political liberty is regarded chiefly as the right to break free from a capitalist state, because, in a socialist society the individual has no desire for liberation from the state. The concept of liberty as

determined by the socialist form of society completely upsets the definition of the rights of man.[34]

Thus, the differences touch the fundamental goals of society. In a closed, authoritarian, Communist society, freedom and the rights of man are clearly limited, according to the philosophic orientation of the state, in order to attain goals which are deemed by the state to be more desirable. Whether or not they are desirable, or what those goals may be, almost become irrelevant when one realizes that, should those who control the state decide to change the goals, postpone them, or do anything else they wish to them, there is no recourse for the individual citizen. He is the captive of his state.

Communist theory does not completely deny the great ideals of recorded history, the ideals to which we are addressing ourselves here. It, too, proclaims its objective to be the equality and brotherhood of mankind. What is new, however, is the bold proclamation that to achieve these goals, the society must close itself to dissent. Attractive as this reasoning may sometimes appear to those who feel no hope under existing conditions, its deception is perilous. History offers little hope that a closed society is capable of overcoming its great weaknesses, the temptations placed before those who control the means of repression to use that control for purposes of maintaining their own power position. The belief that the way to free man from economic exploitation is to suppress the rights of criticism and dissent is sheer illusion, which only makes man vulnerable to new forms of exploitation.

The fundamental premise of a closed society rests in a belief in the omnipotence of man and his capacity to know all there is to know about the world. If certain men cannot have it within their power to know all good, there is no rational justification for closing the society to dissent. Furthermore, it must affirm, and find it palatable, that a few men, by the use of modern techniques of psychology, propaganda, and mass communication, have the power to shape men's minds. A method must be devised to induce men to act and react, consistently, in ways different from their familiar ways of acting, to dispel all the fiercely competitive reactions, to sublimate their aggressions, and to achieve a tolerance and patience heretofore unknown to mankind. If man will not react to this new leadership in a manner similar to Pavlov's dogs, a closed, authoritarian, Communist society, built at the expense of man's freedom and man's blood, can never be a utopia; it can, at best, be an efficient business organization, a good unit of production in which widely different opinions and desires will be repressed in order to expand material power. The difficulties inherent in this approach were discussed by Sigmund Freud:

> The cry for freedom is directed either against particular forms or demands of culture or else against culture itself. It does not seem as if man could be brought by any sort of influence to change his nature into that of the ants; he will always, one imagines, defend his claim to individual freedom against the will of the multitude. A great part of the struggles of mankind centers around the single task of finding some expedient solution between these individual claims and those of the civilized community; it is one of the problems of man's fate whether this solution can be arrived at in some particular form of culture or whether the conflict will prove irreconcilable.[35]

Whether man's restless intellect will ever allow him to be content to follow the course of pure instinct, as may occur in the beehive or anthill, is a critical question for those who advocate the repression of man's freedom for some other ultimate good. Obviously, man's record to date in this regard has not been predictable. Those with such great confidence in man's ability to shape man must be experiencing serious doubts as a result of the visible discord and ennui among the younger generation in the Soviet Union, a generation brought up entirely under Communist training and techniques. What this portends for the future of a utopia that can be built via a closed society is still open to conjecture.

Except for their self-avowed motivation, little difference can be discerned between the closed society today and the feudal and monarchical systems against which mankind struggled for centuries. The basic philosophical orientation of a totalitarian dictatorship is no different from the divine rights of kings. Good kings existed, as did bad, just as some dictatorships proclaim themselves to be good and others are known to all to be tyrannies. Having broken the line of hereditary royal blood upon which the king's pretensions were based, those who seek absolute power today must invoke a different rationalization. Their claim is superior knowledge, based on their exclusive use of scientific reasoning. The fact, however, is that this reasoning is often used to sustain a regime where the people must rely on the benevolence and whim of their rulers for their lives and well-being. Regardless of what claims are made, where the man in opposition is unable to advance his life by the simple means of earning a living, or is impeded from building a good life for himself with a base of power and esteem, as he is able to do in a free society, how free can he be?

While the concept of a guiding elite may be the surest means to a specific objective if the wise men are indeed wise, the facts of human existence are not so permissive. The question always remains: Who is to judge who is wise, and how do you ensure continuity of wisdom in the course of time? This, in essence, is the imperative of democracy.

If mankind's aspirations for individual liberty exist, as they clearly do, it is questionable how long they can be repressed by force or subordinated to other ends. Men who are not free to make their own decisions, but are subject to the unfettered will and rule of other men, are slaves, no matter what other benefits they may derive. They may be allotted several rights; they may have the most benevolent of all governments, but when there is no institution incorporated in the society to

prevent ambitious men from succeeding to power and per-
verting it to their own ends, the people live in the constant
shadow of fear. Should that government withdraw its fiat,
there is no recourse. Without political liberties, man can
never be secure in the protection of his life or his loved ones.

An open society fosters a contrasting atmosphere and environment. With its institutions accessible to all, it encour-
ages in each man a sense of participation, a feeling of security
in that participation, and responsibility for the achievements
and failings of his society. The United States Supreme Court
has described the depth of this participation in the following
terms: "Freedom to differ is not limited to things that do not
matter much. That would be a mere shadow of freedom. The
test of its substance is the right to differ as to things that touch
the heart of the existing order."[36] The freedom to differ is
fomented by the very atmosphere of the society. It is not
something men can be told. The absence of fear is the fundamental prerequisite, whether that be fear of constant observation and spying, of invasion of one's home, of the ultimate
threat to one's very life, or of the basic fear of being unable to
earn a living. It is encouraged by the accessibility of places
immune from the state's authority or presence, where one can
think freely, measuring his inward directions, exploring and
groping for a better life, discussing his thoughts with his intimate associates or in public, or of knowing that there are
other people opposed to the government who have economic
means and will permit him to work productively in a manner
that will be enjoyable to him. This atmosphere may not be
perfect at any particular place or time, but its presence, as an
overriding goal and end of society, fosters a sense of confidence that will help the society to move progressively in the
direction of a better life.

It would certainly be foolish to argue that democracy is a
perfect solution to the evils that we wish to eradicate from the
world. In the face of our inheritance of poverty, illiteracy,

and human beings shorn of their human dignity, there is a difficult road ahead. But rather than accusing democracy of falling short of those goals we seek to attain, let us take a more realistic perspective of history and view ourselves as we advance from the past. Man must walk through history; he cannot jump. The great promises of totalitarian regimes may seem enticing, but they are more likely to produce a step backward rather than a "great leap forward." Although it seems callous to ask the oppressed to be patient, no one has come forth with a better or surer solution to their predicament. Slow, sure steps forward have time and again been proved quicker than the deceptive speed promised by demagogues. W. W. Rostow has demonstrated that the path to economic development is the same sixty years, regardless of what system of government retains control.

Man's government is a means to an end. Should that relationship be confused, it can be fatal. To destroy the essential element of political liberty for the sake of illusory speed in other liberties may be a prelude to great tragedy for countless future generations. With the centralized power of the modern state, and the tendency of absolute power to distort the thinking of those who wield it, we cannot rely on the goodwill of those possessing power to prevent the emergence of a new form of exploitation, which Milovan Djilas of Yugoslavia described so eloquently in his book *The New Class*. Its false promise could place true liberty beyond the reach of mankind for generations to come.

The Rights of Man— And Representative Democracy

The Right to Life, Liberty, and Security

A universally agreed-on definition of the word democracy seems unattainable in our imperfect world. Yet the disagreement on that subject is like a tender lover's quarrel compared to the disputes which arise when one attempts to identify its specific elements. It is not expected that this attempt will be any different. Lack of agreement, however, is a feeble excuse for inaction. Accordingly, in this second part, our purpose is to identify those civil and political rights which are integrally related to the effective operation of a representative democracy and, in each instance, to analyze the nature of that relationship.

Not all human rights are equally important to the functioning of self-government. The role of some is more easily identifiable than others. They all, however, are deeply interrelated. It would be difficult, if not impossible, to operate a government which seeks to know and reflect the wishes of the governed without invoking most, if not all, of the civil and political rights. With these as a minimum, there is some hope of going on to obtain other social and economic benefits as a functional result of self-government. Without these, the others alone promise to be short-lived.

Democracy, as we have defined it, is a complex interaction of forces, all of which must be enabled to operate with reasonable freedom from arbitrary restraint. To secure that freedom, we consider that the citizens of a state must be fully confident that the following rights will be operative: the right to life, liberty, and security, under which are included freedom of movement, the right to due process of law, freedom from arbitrary arrest, and the right to privacy; equal protection of the laws; the right to free assembly and association; the right to peaceful petition; freedom of thought and expression; the right to the protection of impartial courts, which includes the right to a fair trial, and freedom from *ex post facto* laws; and, finally, the right to an education. Many might want to add to this list; it is virtually impossible to subtract from it and leave any meaning to the word democracy.

Life, liberty, and security need no explanation. They are the fundamental precepts of any system of human rights. It is to secure them that "governments are instituted among men." All universal declarations of human rights incorporate them; all the American states recognize their essential nature and guarantee their protection.[1] The reports of the United Nations characterize life as the "minimum human right" which "no government has the right to deny arbitrarily."[2] Immanuel Kant described liberty as the "one sole original inborn right belonging to every man in virtue of his humanity."[3] Security is not an abstract concept, but refers directly to the principles of life and liberty, and to the atmosphere of the society which engenders confidence in their safe enjoyment. As Montesquieu affirmed, "Political liberty consists in security, or at least in the opinion that we enjoy security."[4]

The ideal of security in life and in liberty dates back, of

course, far earlier than the philosophers of the eighteenth and nineteenth centuries and the American and French revolutions. It permeates all man's history, some philosophers tracing its roots to the kingdom of animals. A broad concept, touching every aspect of man's existence, it has been described in this manner:

> The right to personal security emanates in a person's legal and uninterrupted enjoyment of his life, his limbs, his body, his health, and his reputation. It includes the right to exist, and the right to enjoyment of life while existing, and it is invaded not only by a deprivation of life but also by a deprivation of those things which are necessary to the enjoyment of life according to the nature, temperament, and lawful desires of the individual.[5]

The true nature of liberty under government has long been a subject of philosophic inquiry. Where liberty has been denied to be an effective means of attaining the goal of a happy and full life, democracy has likewise been condemned as an inferior method of government. Their negation has gone hand in hand. The philosopher-king of Plato's *Republic*, for example, ruled over a rigidly, albeit "rationally," structuralized society, where each person was limited to a determined sphere of action. Marx and Engels envisaged an educated, indoctrinated elite guiding and directing the society to its ideal realizations. In contrast, Aristotle considered the concept from the perspective of relativity. While democracy may not be the most perfect form of government, he concluded that it was also least likely to be the worst; while it could be most lethargic in enacting positive measures to improve life and liberty, it was least likely to run roughshod over these precious rights.

Obviously, the liberty sought under democratic government is different from that obtained in a state of nature, which is not so encumbered with responsibilities and obligations. Liberty carried to the extreme can destroy security. Thus,

while security is necessary in order for a people to be truly free, freedom cannot be considered the license of some to abolish the security of others. Where liberty and security are concomitant values, the rule of law is recognized as an equally important element of the society, to ensure that the exercise of the liberty of one remains consistent with that of his neighbor. In modern society, liberty is attainable only under the rule of law; whether it is attainable depends on the nature of those laws. This is precisely why the right to liberty is not only a fundamental condition of democracy; democracy is a condition of liberty. Just as law is prerequisite to preserving man's liberty against infringement by others in the exercise of their liberty, so democracy is essential to ensure that the law will fulfill that function. By placing ultimate control of the law in the hands of the many, we accept the proposition that an educated and enlightened citizenry, with an equal voice for all, is least likely to abuse its power. The need for persuasion and debate before action reduces to a minimum the possibility of precipitate action against liberties. Difficulties do arise where the natural operation of certain institutions, whether economic or social, gives one group an advantage over another, and positive government action is required as a counterbalance. Also, the requirements of discussion and deliberation often impede the immediate redress of injustice. It is here, however, that the other institutions of self-help and self-government, such as the power of publicity, the force of elections, and the ambition of certain men to achieve self-advancement by publicizing the grievances of minorities, come into play. The alternative—relying on the benevolence of one group to correct the injustices—has historically been almost a total failure.

By the same token, however, democracy cannot function unless her citizens feel themselves secure in their life and liberty. Fearful men cannot act in their own or the common interest as they themselves perceive that interest. Not only

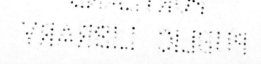

the words of the constitution, but the very atmosphere of a democracy must breed confidence in personal security. Thus, the equation is this. Life without liberty, however you define that liberty, is meaningless. Without security, liberty is a fiction, and security permeates all levels and all phases of human existence. Without the security to act freely, man cannot be relied upon to act and vote, in the majority of instances, in his own best interests or in the interests of the majority of his society. Unless man is doing this, democracy is a sham. Thus, respect for life, liberty, and security, to the exclusion or derogation of none of these elements, is fundamental to man's existence and prerequisite to the effective exercise of representative democracy.

FREEDOM OF MOVEMENT

The right to freedom of movement is widely recognized.[6] In the tradition of the common law and democracy as practiced in the United States, it has been considered to be of the first rank and an integral part of liberty. The courts have declared that: "The right of personal liberty is fundamental . . . and one of the most sacred and valuable rights. It consists of the power of locomotion without restraint except by due process."[7]

Justice William O. Douglas of the United States Supreme Court has stated that:

> The right to travel is a part of the "liberty" of which the citizen could not be deprived without due process of law. . . . In Anglo-Saxon law that right was emerging at least as early as the Magna Carta (Article 42). . . . Freedom of movement across frontiers in either direction, and inside frontiers as well, was a part of our heritage. Travel abroad, like travel within the country, may be necessary for a livelihood. It may be as close to the heart of the individual as the choice of what he eats, or wears, or reads. Freedom of movement is basic in our scheme of values.[8]

Although it may have been argued in the past that a democracy could function without granting unrestricted freedom of movement, and the matter of foreign travel to unfriendly states will always be a problem, the preservation of responsive government and the other basic human rights in the modern world depends on it. The activities of government, spanning a wide area, if arbitrarily abused, constitute the principal threat to the full enjoyment of liberty. This area must be accessible to reporters, writers, and lecturers to know and gather information firsthand without having to rely on what others relate to them. Freedom of movement is necessary to science, to scholarship, to the proper conduct of public affairs, and it is vital to a comfortable and happy life. In short, in a democracy, it is an element in the atmosphere of security; its citizens cannot be confident unless they know that those members of their society who wish to and need to move about freely are able to do so.

Its intimate relationship to military security makes this right one of the first to meet with restriction in time of national emergency. In the constitutional provisions for a state of siege, the principal restriction to individual liberty concerns the curtailing of freedom of movement; this provision is contained in almost every American constitution.[9] For similar reasons of national security, many democratic states exercise control over the freedom of movement when it entails the crossing of national borders. While many of these restrictions are justified by the problem of the survival of democracy, in the face of an anarchical international system, such restraints are not without substantial dangers to the ability of the citizen to remain fully informed and aware of problems confronting his nation. Self-deception is incompatible with self-government. These restrictions highlight the importance of the freedom of movement to a true state of liberty, inasmuch as its denial is one of the principal security measures of the regime which must maintain its will by force and repression. On the other hand, the inability of a democratic government, which respects human rights, to impose such measures surreptitiously, is what enables the people living under such a government to protect themselves against the invasion of their essential civil rights.

DUE PROCESS OF LAW

We have observed that liberty is a fundamental element of representative democracy, that the people must be secure in their knowledge of their liberty, and that security must be grounded in substantial safeguards. To declare that a people are free, and that liberty reigns in a country, is meaningless unless some institution is incorporated in the basic organization of the society to ensure to each individual citizen that his liberty is secure. Such an institution must be rooted in easy access to adequate and effective remedies when liberty is violated. One cannot stop men or governments from violating the liberties of citizens, but one can provide citizens with adequate remedies when such events occur.

Equally important, as will be noted in the discussion of limitations on these rights, occasions do arise in a democracy when it is necessary, temporarily, to restrain the citizen's enjoyment of his liberties. In this event, adequate and effective remedies for violations are essential. Those remedies, which are embodied in the rule of law and termed due process of law, are the only protections left to the citizen in this contingency. They must never be withdrawn at the risk of losing all. The United States Constitution is explicit on this point. A man may be deprived of his liberty, the Fourteenth Amendment states, but only by due process of law. In other words, if liberty is ever to be restricted, the necessity must be clearly demonstrated according to pre-established procedures.

The people must have confidence in the remedies afforded to them. All the protection imaginable is useless if, in demanding their rights, they must fear for their lives, loved ones, or possessions. Again, there must be an atmosphere in which the people feel safe to demand their rightful remedies. That atmosphere can be engendered only where governmental power is circumscribed by rules of law which preclude the arbitrary exercise of that power and afford the citizen ample opportunity to contest the validity of those measures taken against him. This is implicit in an enduring, ordered scheme of liberty. This rule of law is essential to ensure the confidence of the people that those of his fellow citizens whom he has entrusted with the task of administering the government, and maintaining law and order, remain responsible to the community and that they do not abuse those powers. An interesting analogy in describing this requirement of man's feeling of security was made by Sigmund Freud: "I hardly think that any of us would be willing even to enter a motor car, if the driver informed us that he drove without allowing himself to be distracted by traffic regulations, but in accordance with the impulses of an exalted imagination."[10] In the long run, only the constant check provided by a system of government in which the ultimate power remains securely in the hands of the people can ensure observance of the rule of law.

In the Western world, that restraint on the arbitrary exercise of governmental power is known as the due process of law. Due process, however, is a broad term, with both substantive and adjective applications. In substantive form it means that the law of the society, as enacted by the state, cannot violate specific safeguards or deprive a person of life or liberty without following lawful procedures and affording the individual every possible protection against arbitrary and unjust acts. In its procedural formulations, it refers to those elements of protection afforded to the individual to defend himself before the courts of justice. In this section we shall consider the substantive right; when we discuss the judicial guarantees we shall examine the procedural aspect of due process.

In its substantive form, due process has received universal recognition as an element of democratic institutions.[11] It is, in essence, the embodiment of the rule of law and has roots deep in the history of man, antedating the Magna Carta.[12] Although it is difficult to define, its procedural aspects were eloquently described in a manner applicable here. It is, in the words of Justice Benjamin N. Cardozo of the United States Supreme Court, designed to prevent state action which "offends some principle of justice so rooted in the traditions and conscience of our people as to be ranked as fundamental,"[13] and is "implicit in the concept of ordered liberty."[14] Justice Felix Frankfurter of the United States Supreme Court said of it: "Due process of law conveys neither formal nor fixed nor narrow requirements. It is the compendious expression for all those rights which the courts must enforce because they are basic to our free society. . . . It is of the very nature of a free society to advance in its standards of what is deemed reasonable and right."[15]

In essence, then, the concept embraces respect and protection for all other human rights, and obligates the legislature and the executive to observe fundamental canons of decency, fairness, and justice. It means that the law advanced by legislative bodies must follow certain procedures, be well-grounded and well-defined so that the citizen can know what is expected of him and what is not. In this respect it is the underpinning of all other human rights. If law is nothing more than the ground rules by which the men in a society operate, due process sets the ground rules by which law is enacted. It helps to protect the citizen from harm, even from the majorities in a democratic government. Those who, because of past deprivations, proclaim that there is not time for due process, are saying in effect that there is not time for democracy, that there is not time for the will of the people. For without due process, the law of the democracy becomes that of the loudest, most boisterous, roughest element of the society. Without it no safeguards will exist to prevent the majority from running roughshod over the minorities, only to establish the principle that the minorities must act in similar fashion to secure their rights by destroying a tyrannical democracy of a majority. Due process is the protection for the entire framework of the democratic process, with equal rights and guarantees, and equal consideration for all its component elements. It thus enables the citizen to guide his own conduct and to weigh and discuss the functioning of his government, and the directions of his society, without the fear and uncertainty that comes from a government that arbitrarily establishes new rules.

ARBITRARY ARREST AND DETENTION

One aspect of the due process of law elemental to liberty is freedom from arbitrary arrest and detention.[16] It is of crucial importance that citizens know that arrest or detention cannot be arbitrarily applied at the discretion or pleasure of the executive authority. Unless the citizens are secure in this right, a pall is cast over all other rights. Should the possibility of arbitrary arrest exist, all other restraints upon the action of government become empty hopes, and democracy cannot benefit by the free and unfettered judgment of the people upon whom it must depend to direct its proper conduct.

Blackstone, in his famous *Commentaries*, signaled the danger:

> if it were left in the power of any, the highest magistrate to imprison arbitrarily whomever he or his officers thought improper, there would soon be an end of all other rights and immunities. . . . To bereave a man of life, or by violence to confiscate his estate, without accusation or trial, would be so gross and notorious an act of despotism, as would at once convey the alarm of tyranny throughout the whole kingdom; but confinement of the person, by secretly hurrying him to gaol, where his suffer-

ings are unknown or forgotten, is a less public, a less striking, and therefore a more dangerous engine of arbitrary government.[17]

Historically, the abuses of this right need no footnote. The use of arbitrary arrest to extract confessions, hold a person incommunicado from family and friends, without advice of counsel, and without effective limits on the time or methods of interrogation, are well known. Even where public trial is permitted at a later time, its evils are irremediable, since abuses during detention, involving the word of an accused against a public official, are difficult to prove.

The perils of this situation may not seem real to citizens who have confidence in their government, and may thus permit the loosening of requirements for arrest for known criminals. But it is precisely to remove all opportunities from those men who might be tempted to abuse their public trust that this protection is essential even for those persons who, by the consensus of society, are dangerous. For the essential question is: Who is to judge guilt, and upon what evidence? It has been well stated that: "Before trial we cannot have one rule for innocent prisoners and another rule for guilty prisoners, because we do not know which are which until the verdict of conviction is given. . . . The function of sifting the innocent from the guilty must not be usurped by the police, no matter how able and devoted they are."[18]

The recollection of how law-abiding Social Democrats disappeared overnight when the Nazis assumed power in Germany is sufficient to warn us of the dangers of these procedures, not to speak of the recent example of Fidel Castro's Cuba, where the absence of restraint on state power and the recognition of economic crimes have subjected thousands of citizens to arbitrary "justice."[19]

The rules which protect the individual's right to be free from such action on the part of those to whom he has entrusted public power are the rules of due process of law. In this area they dictate that no arrest or imprisonment can be effected unless (1) a warrant is issued for that arrest, (2) by a competent authority, (3) for good cause, (4) based upon a pre-existing law, and (5) the individual arrested has the right to challenge the legality of that arrest without delay. These procedures are important to all levels of society. As stated by Justice Frankfurter:

> Legislation . . . requiring that the police must with reasonable promptness show legal cause for detaining arrested persons, constitutes an important safeguard—not only in assuring protection for the innocent but also in securing conviction of the guilty by methods that commend themselves to a progressive and self-confident society.[20]

Various means exist for attaining this end within the framework of an operating democracy. One solution employed in the Federal Courts of the United States is to deny the admissibility of any evidence secured as a result of arbitrary detention.

The most effective of these remedies, however, are those for immediate summary judicial review (habeas corpus) and the writ of *amparo* (employed in the legal codes of many Latin American countries), both of which seek the same end: to guarantee that the citizen shall not be deprived of his liberty without prompt, impartial review of the charges made against him, according to the rule of law. The importance of this remedy is illustrated in the fact that in the United States Constitution its restriction is prohibited except under situations of great danger to the nation.[21] A number of other American constitutions prohibit even that limited restriction. As critical as these protections are, however, the citizen can be secure in the knowledge of their efficacy only in a democracy, where power is not absolute and numerous restraints on public power exist, including an independent judiciary to check the executive, and to safeguard freedom from arbitrary arrest.

THE RIGHT TO PRIVACY:
THE INVIOLABILITY OF THE HOME

At times, it has been questioned whether the right to privacy—or, as it has sometimes been characterized, the "right to be let alone"—is a primary right absolutely essential to the effective functioning of a democratic society.[22] It seems clear, however, that the atmosphere of freedom and security of action, without which men are unable to function effectively in a democracy, cannot be engendered without the right to privacy. U.S. Supreme Court Justice Louis D. Brandeis phrased it in this way:

> The makers of our Constitution undertook to secure conditions favorable to the pursuit of happiness. They recognized the significance of man's spiritual nature, of his feelings and of his intellect. They knew that only a part of the pain, pleasure, and satisfactions of life are to be found in material things. They sought to protect Americans in their beliefs, their thoughts, their emotions, and their sensations. They conferred, as against the Government, the right to be let alone—the most comprehensive of rights and the right most valued by civilized men.[23]

In another decision, the United States Supreme Court, speaking through Justice Frankfurter, said:

> The security of one's privacy against intrusion by the police . . . is basic to a free society. . . . The knock at the door, whether by day or by night, as a prelude to a search, without authority of the police, did not need the commentary of recent history to be condemned as inconsistent with the conception of human rights enshrined in the history and the basic constitutional doctrine of the English speaking peoples.[24]

The arbitrary invasion of the privacy of individual citizens, without the authority of law, is only more obnoxious to freedom than specific laws permitted in the society which infringe the individual's privacy. From colonial times, when businesses and homes could be searched at any time, without any reasonable indication that the person involved was violating a law, until today, when opponents of totalitarian regimes are terrorized, it has been and is evident that democracy cannot function in such an atmosphere.

But more important is the converse relationship. The protection of the right of privacy can be secure only in a democracy where power is not absolute and the guarantees of judicial protection exist. If the full freedoms of a democracy are functioning, no man's privacy can be invaded while his neighbors and fellow citizens claim ignorance or impotence.

This right is sometimes difficult to enforce in a society. It may operate to enable antisocial criminals to escape punishment because evidence against them cannot be gathered except surreptitiously. Citizens are often stirred to become militant and irrational in their attitudes when a known criminal cannot be prosecuted. Although this is understandable, it must also be appreciated that the enforcement of the right of privacy does not make the society incapable of proceeding against lawbreakers. It is essential to all men, however, and especially to the innocent, to secure the warrant of disinterested and independent judicial authorities before a citizen's privacy can be violated, and not to place discretion in the hands of arbitrary political authorities. It is far more dangerous to the survival of a democracy when innocent men run the risk of having the security of their privacy taken away from them without due process of law than it is to have an occasional criminal go unpunished. That criminal who must go free because the society is unable to marshal sufficient evidence against him may cause great harm, even tragedy, to individual citizens of the society. This is certainly not a comforting thought. But if we sanction the derogation of the right of privacy to avoid this one evil, the potential abuses can lead to far greater evils, and even to the destruction of the democracy from within.

The problem becomes more acute when the need arises to take action against those who we know are seeking to destroy democratic institutions. Numerous constitutions expressly sanction the derogation of this right, in situations of national emergency, under a state of siege.[25] Whether the protection gained thereby for the democracy is real or illusory is answered when one considers the grave abuses recorded of this authority honestly given. How much faith should a citizen have that his government will act in accordance with the spirit of free institutions? If we could rely on faith, we could do away with most of the safeguards for democratic institutions which are embodied in the constitutional rights. With respect to the disregard of privacy in order to protect democracy, it has been observed: "To a Communist society, such a system is appropriate; it protects Communism. To a free society, it can never be appropriate; it does not protect freedom, it destroys it."[26]

The whole purpose of a democracy is to create the institutions which enable a citizen's faith in his government to be grounded in realistic knowledge. The apparent necessity for measures granting arbitrary powers to government officials, to invade privacy in certain circumstances, can establish the type of precedent which may be distorted and turned against true freedom at any time. When one considers that democracy is not without protection, that the laws of a democracy permit punishment against overt acts and against covert acts which can be proved according to legal proceedings, the urgency for this type of protection clearly diminishes. When considered in relation to the abuses which in fact consistently emanate from it in history, the advisability of tolerating intrusion into privacy is reduced even further. The real question which any society must face is, who is to decide which persons are the threat to the survival of the society? The possible abuse of the right to make this decision compels a democracy to insist on proper procedure and protection, whenever it appears necessary to invade the privacy of one of its citizens. Only thus may men have confidence in their institutions, and act accordingly.

Equal Protection of the Laws

The corollary to the principle that all men are born with equal rights, affirmed in the Universal and the American declarations of rights,[27] is that all men are entitled to receive equal protection from the laws of their government.[28] If democracy is to benefit from the effective participation of all its citizens in the conduct of its affairs, an essential prerequisite to that participation is that the laws of the state do not discriminate between its citizens. This principle underlies all international formulations of human rights and is embodied in the constitutions of all the American republics.

Similar to due process of law, this right is distinguishable in two phases, the substantive and the procedural recognition of the right of the citizen to equal protection. In substance, it guarantees that all citizens shall be treated as equals, without being discriminated against in the law of the state or in the decrees of the legislature and the executive. In its procedural aspect, it refers not to the substance of the law, but to the manner in which it is applied and administered by the executive and judicial branches of government.

In its substantive aspect, it was defined by the International Commission of Jurists in the following terms:

> The law passed by the legislature must not discriminate between human beings except insofar as such discrimination can be justified on a rational classification consistent with the progressive enhancement of human dignity within a particular society.[29]

The United States Supreme Court has declared that "equal protection of the laws is a pledge of the protection of equal laws."[30] It is a guarantee:

> that all persons subjected to state legislation shall be treated alike, under like circumstances and conditions, both in privileges conferred and in liabilities imposed. . . . It is intended to secure and safeguard equality of right and of treatment against intentional and arbitrary discrimination.[31]

The relationship to the effective functioning of a democracy is elemental. A citizen is unlikely to have an interest in the preservation of the law and order of the society unless he receives consideration from that society equal to that accorded to all other members. To the extent that he is discriminated against, he will seek, if possible, to change the rule of that society. Depending on the number of people in a similar status, their articulateness, and their determination, this can have serious consequences, culminating, in the extreme, in rebellion and revolution. As Harold Laski has stated: "It is a pretty fair historical generalization to say that no right is likely to have effective operation in any society unless the citizens of that society have a broadly equal interest in the results of its fulfillment."[32] Thus, the equal treatment of all citizens by the law of their society is basic to maintaining their desire to respect the laws and mandates of that society.

Equality of treatment is critical in all matters affecting the public, whether it be laws affecting commerce and taxation, or discrimination on racial, religious, or ethnic grounds. Discrimination against any group is, of course, inimical to the practice of true democracy, which, by definition, reflects the will of all the people. Not that discrimination will not be practiced among individual citizens in a democracy. It will. Unfortunately, mankind has far to go before he is able to overcome this malady in his personal life. Discrimination that has the sanction of the laws of the state, however, and authorizes special treatment for different groups of society, on no other grounds but that the group is "different," is establishing a precedent that can be readily distorted to destroy democracy. Once the principle of exceptions from enjoyment of these basic rights is made, once the line is drawn to include some human beings and exclude others, it ceases to be a matter of principle but becomes a matter of discretion as to where the line should be drawn. Those who are on one side of the line today cannot be heard to complain because the line is shifted and tomorrow, when the balance of power alters, they are on the other side of a new line drawn with different criteria. This applies alike to those who would draw lines on racial grounds, on political grounds, or, as the Marxist-oriented ideologies do, on economic grounds.

The respect for all segments of the society, regardless of their differing views, is grounded in a very pragmatic principle: the self-interest of each group to belong to a society which permits it to express its values and to work to convince other men to influence the directions of the society according to its convictions. If we are unwilling to risk this and seek to draw lines for our purposes today, we must be willing to bear the consequences of establishing the principle that those lines of exclusion can be drawn. All citizens have a strong interest in maintaining this mechanism, for those who belong to today's majority may readily find themselves in tomorrow's minority.

The right of equal protection of the laws must be established as a principle above the ordinary law of the society, as a fundamental right of man. This is of compelling importance. Its violation, of course, is most pernicious to a thriving democracy when it impedes certain groups from expressing themselves and protecting their rights. This touches the very heart of their right to participate in government. The right to a ballot has little meaning to a person prevented from persuading others of the merits of joining with him. Although subject to the exception that the interpretation of equal protection cannot impede the legitimate exercise of the police power by the state, the exercise of that power must apply equally and uniformly to all citizens and not single out any group for special treatment, unless such a group can be shown to present a clear danger to the maintenance of order in the society.[33]

In its procedural aspects, equal protection proscribes the administration and application of the law so as to favor or discriminate against any citizen or group of citizens. This is, in essence, the meaning of the word justice. Not only must the law of the society treat all citizens as equals, but when each citizen petitions the courts and other institutions of the society for protection, persons entrusted with manning those courts and institutions must ascertain that the spirit of the law is not broken in favor of or against any individual.

The second consequence of drawing distinctions between the rights of different citizens, and failing to respect the interests of the whole society, was well expressed by Justice Hugo L. Black of the United States Supreme Court:

> Centuries of experience testify that laws aimed at one political or religious group, however rational these laws may be in their beginnings, generate hatreds and prejudice which rapidly spread beyond control. Too often it is fear which inspires such passions, and nothing is more reckless or contagious. . . . Under such circumstances, restrictions imposed on proscribed groups are seldom static, even though the rate of expansion may not move in geometric progression. . . . Today the "political affiliation" happens to be the Communist Party. . . . Under this reasoning, affiliation with other political parties can be proscribed just as validly. Guilt should not be imputed solely from association or affiliation with political parties or any other organization, however much we abhor the ideas which they advocate. Like anyone else, individual Communists who commit overt acts in violation of valid laws can and should be

punished. But the postulate of the First Amendment is that our free institutions can be maintained without proscribing or penalizing political belief, speech, press, assembly, or party affiliation. This is a far bolder philosophy than despotic rulers can afford to follow. It is the heart of the system on which our freedom depends.[34]

In part, this "bolder" freedom "than despotic rulers can afford to follow" is based on the assumption that, given an equal opportunity, true ideas will triumph over false ideas. But while truth can triumph over falsehood, truth cannot triumph over persecution. John Stuart Mill stated that "the dictum that truth always triumphs over persecution is one of those pleasant falsehoods which men repeat . . . till they pass into commonplace, but which all experience refutes. History teems with instances of truth put down by persecution." Thus, if the principle of persecution is tolerated in any form, if society fails to recognize its duty to all groups of that society, the fundamental philosophic underpinnings of democratic progress—the idea that a well-informed body politic will be able to conduct its affairs for the well-being of all—is placed at a grave disadvantage. This was clearly characterized by Justice Black when he said that "equal protection to all is the basic principle upon which justice under law rests."[35] Sigmund Freud, in an analysis of the discontent of society, even defined the word justice in terms of this concept. He said:

> This substitution of the power of a united number for the power of a single man is the decisive step towards civilization. . . . The first requisite of culture, therefore, is justice—that is the assurance that a law once made will not be broken in favor of any individual. This implies nothing about the ethical value of any such law.[36]

The real danger of frustrating this cherished goal in a democracy arises not solely from those who would usurp power

for their own ends, but when a clear and cohesive majority
seeks to discriminate against a minority. It would be absurd
to claim that the "people can do no wrong," and no one even
vaguely acquainted with history would dare to do so. Irrational prejudices among a mass of people are easily engendered, a familiar occurrence in racial matters; today this has
become fashionable, among some groups, in economic matters,
as is evident in the class antagonisms that are stirred by Marxist-oriented ideologies. The sanction of the equal protection
of the laws in a democracy, however, is an attempt to create
an unalterable mechanism to safeguard the security of minorities and dissenters to the extent that this is possible in human
affairs.

The aim of democracy is to achieve justice among men. It
must do this for all its citizens, or it fails to be an effective
government for all its citizens. Conversely, the practices and
habits of democracy contribute most effectively to the attainment of the concept of equal protection of the laws, for only
in a government where absolute power cannot be concentrated in the hands of one man or a small group of men, can
this right ultimately be secured. This right can be secure only
in that form of government where every citizen has equal access to participation in his government and can, directly and
in combination with other citizens, insist on an equal share in
the benefits of society, without having to rely on the whim or
benevolence of any particular person or group to assure him
fair and equal treatment.

The Right of Assembly and Association

The right of assembly and the right of association are intimately linked. By the latter, a citizen is free to associate
with whom he chooses, without being subject to penalty in
the exercise of his other civil, political, economic, or social
rights because of that association. It includes the right to form

associations as well as the right to join existing associations, and encompasses all phases of life in a modern world. It is most relevant to the exercise of representative democracy when it embraces political rights and the right to form or to join political associations for the purpose of advancing certain ideas or opinions in the political life of the nation. The right of assembly is the right to gather in groups, public or private, to discuss or petition for those ideas. These rights are contained in all of the international declarations and drafts and in the constitutions of all the American states.

They have long been considered fundamental to the functioning of a democracy and to the effective mobilization of the citizens of a democracy to proclaim and assert their rights and interests as they understand them.[37] When the United States was scarcely a century old, in 1875, the Supreme Court declared:

> The right of people peaceably to assemble for lawful purposes existed long before the adoption of the Constitution of the United States. In fact, it is, and always has been, one of the attributes of citizenship under a free government. . . . It is found wherever civilization exists. . . . The very idea of a government, republican in form, implies a right on the part of its citizens to meet peaceably for consultation in respect to public affairs and to petition for a redress of grievances.[38]

Chief Justice Earl Warren, of the Supreme Court of the United States, elaborated on this right in the decision limiting the scope of inquiry of the Un-American Activities Committee:

> A fundamental principle of a democratic society is political freedom of the individual. Our form of government is built on the premise that every citizen shall have the right to engage in political expression and association. . . . Exercise of these basic freedoms in America has traditionally been through media of political associations. Any interference with the free-

dom of a party is simultaneously an interference with the freedom of its adherents. . . . History has amply proved the virtue of political activity by minority, dissident groups, who innumerable times have been in the vanguard of democratic thought and whose programs were ultimately accepted.[39]

Democracy feeds and thrives upon the thought and action of its citizens. To act upon one's thoughts in a democracy implies bringing those thoughts to the attention of the government, which can be effectively done only in combination with other citizens. To stifle the association and assembly of citizens is to suppress the source of ideas of the very people who are to be governed. The Mexican philosopher Antonio Caso pointed out, in 1941, the almost exclusive identification of this type of activity with democracy: "There is another liberty essential in the life of nations, that of political association and in forms other than those provided by the state itself, for it is not the only social form. Totalitarianism fails to recognize this."[40] The right to associate freely extends not only to political rights. It is clearly evident in the right of workers to associate in unions to further their economic interests, or in the right of minorities, who sense discrimination, to make their collective will known.

The entire concept of human rights is fortified by the maintenance of the right to association and assembly because, next to actual participation in the processes of government through the ballot, it is one of the most effective means to publicize the grievances of the citizenry. In the form of uniting in political associations, it ensures the effectiveness of the ballot. In the last analysis, it can hardly be denied by government, since its culmination is in association for revolution. The concentrated power of government, with modern arms at its disposal, however, makes its exercise in this extreme every day more difficult, especially when a government is well organized and intent on denying these rights.

This dramatizes, all the more, why this right is an essential hallmark of a democratic society, which should neither fear nor suffer from, but rather seek and benefit from the associations and public airing of grievances by its citizens.

The exercise of these rights does, however, present risks to the state and to the functioning of democracy which cannot be lightly passed over. Certain groups of citizens may seek to assemble for the express purpose of denying other groups their rights under law. Here is not the threat of majority action, which might take a more political form of expression, but of one minority bringing pressure against other minorities. Hence, when this right is considered, it is inevitably considered with exceptions permitted for the safety and welfare of the public. Such restrictions and limits to this right are encountered in the draft international conventions pertaining to this subject,[41] and are considered necessary for a democratic government to protect itself against the physical force, violence, and lawlessness which can emerge from the abuse of this right.

The power of the state to restrict the right, however, is subject to important limitations in order to prevent abuses from that quarter. This is due to the intimate relationship of the right of assembly and association with the right of freedom of expression. Although some measure of control must be maintained by the police power of the state in the interest of law and order, and the "peace and quiet of the community," those controls must be clearly defined and severely limited to specific problems which are readily identifiable. As Justice Douglas has warned:

> The police power of local government can reach such things as noise, riots, and traffic jams. It cannot, however, reach freedom of expression. If, therefore, a meeting, a lecture, or a speech presents problems of noise, riots, or traffic jams the latter can be regulated even in the form of licensing. But lest the regulation in the interest of noise, riot, or traffic control be used as a cloak to control freedom of expression or have that effect, the

Court has insisted that the regulation be "narrowly drawn to prevent the supposed evil."[42]

As an example of broad prohibitions on freedom of assembly and association, it was proposed in the United Nations to permit a state to exclude fascist and antidemocratic organizations from enjoyment of these rights. The danger from the lack of clear definition of these terms, and the possible perversion of their ends according to the whim and fad of the day, was evident, and such license was rejected.[43]

The Right to Peaceful Petition

Whether the right to peaceful petition ought to be considered as a distinct right, or whether it is, in fact, an extension of the right to assembly and the right to free speech, has been subject to question. There is, after all, no set form for a petition, no courts or procedure which must be followed. Unless some means exist of ascertaining that it has fair consideration, a petition as such is of limited utility. If a grievance may effectively be brought to the attention of the government, through the normal means of communication, it is redundant, it is argued, to categorize this as an individual right. The very right to participate in government through one's chosen representatives, the hallmark of democracy, implies the right to petition through those representatives.

The right was omitted from the Universal Declaration of Human Rights, principally because the delegates felt that it would be too difficult to implement. It was, however, the subject of Resolution 217B (III) of the United Nations General Assembly, in which it was characterized as a "fundamental human right." Although incorporated in the American Declaration of the Rights and Duties of Man, it has not been included in the American and United Nations draft conventions and covenants.

The right has a long history and has played a significant

role in the development of human freedom in the West. Drost has defined it as enabling:

> the individual to address the national authorities with impunity on problems, personal or general, which are usually not of a legal nature. The petition deals mostly with political, economic, or social matters, for which no judicial redress exists because they usually rest within governmental discretion.[44]

John Milton, in his historic defense of freedom of speech, the *Areopagitica,* related it to the right of petition, stating:

> that no grievance ever should arise in the Commonwealth, that let no man in this World expect; but when complaints are freely heard, deeply considered, and speedily reformed, then is the utmost bound of civil liberty attained, that wise men look for.

Although the right of petition is sanctioned in the constitutions of many countries, little is said of the procedure to be followed in its implementation.[45] It is guaranteed in the abstract, and herein lies the difficulty in relating it to the functioning of a viable democracy. Basically, where democratic government is effectively operating, so that the rights of assembly and speech are fully guaranteed, that same spirit will carry over into this field, and the right of petition will automatically be secured. Where respect for these other human rights is not present, then the most elaborate guarantees of the right to petition will not prevent the government from receiving the petition, according it full respect and elaborate procedural guarantees, and yet doing nothing about the matter.

In sum, this right is basic to the exercise of democracy. Its promotion and furtherance alone, however, without giving thought as to how it may lead to effective, impartial, substantive implementation, is no material addition to the ultimate control the people have over their representatives in the normal exercise of representative democracy.

Freedom of Thought, Speech, Expression, and the Press

Although the freedoms of thought, speech, expression, and the press are not identical, they are so intimately related in their function in a democratic, free society, that we shall treat them here as one, indivisible right.[46]

The concept of freedom of thought and expression underlies all thought and writings on the effective functioning of democratic government. Dating back to ancient Greece and Rome, it is today uniformly expressed in the modern constitutional democracies.[47] It was the reason for Milton's *Areopagitica,* in which he stated, "Give me the liberty to know, to utter and to argue freely according to the conscience, above all liberties." The French Declaration of the Rights of Man added emphasis in the assertion that "The free communication of ideas and opinions is one of the most precious of the rights of man." In recent times, Justice Cardozo called it "the matrix, the indispensable condition of nearly every other form of freedom."[48] This aspect was underscored in the United Nations debates where it was characterized as the "touchstone of all the freedoms to which the United Nations is consecrated," referring to all the economic and social rights and guarantees.[49] It has also been singled out for special citation in a number of inter-American conferences as "of the innermost essence of democracy."[50]

The fundamental nature of this right for the effective exercise of representative democracy derives from the nature of the world and the place of man in it. No matter how innately wise and well-motivated a man may be, his decisions and his vote can be no better than his sources of information. If men are to govern themselves, the only manner of effectively doing so is to be well informed about the issues that confront them. All the good judgment in the world is useless if the sources of information are inadequate.

Thus, the basic and absolute need for freedom of expression is that it alone can ensure the progress of a society which relies on the decisions of its citizens to direct its course. The individual human being is the stuff of a democracy; to reduce the effectiveness of any individual by failing to provide him with the resources to make a full and informed decision in his own and the community's interest is not only to squander the natural resource of democratic government, but to incapacitate the ultimate decision-maker in the democratic process. Democracy cannot function without free expression.

This fundamental relationship has been eloquently expressed on innumerable occasions. It seems appropriate to pause to examine a few. Justice Douglas has stated:

> Free speech has occupied an exalted position because of the high service it has given to our society. Its protection is essential to the very existence of a democracy. The airing of ideas releases pressures which otherwise might become destructive. When ideas compete in the market for acceptance, full and free discussion exposes the false and they gain few adherents. . . . Full and free discussion keeps a society from becoming stagnant and unprepared for the stresses and strains that work to tear all civilizations apart. Full and free discussion has indeed been the first article of our faith.[51]

Alexander Meiklejohn said:

> When men govern themselves it is they, and no one else who must pass judgment upon unwisdom, and unfairness and danger. And that means that unwise ideas must have a hearing as well as wise ones, unfair as well as fair, dangerous as well as safe. . . . Just so far as, at any point, the citizens who are to decide an issue are denied acquaintance with information or doubt or disbelief or criticism which is relevant to that issue, just so far the result must be ill-considered, ill-balanced planning for the general good. . . . The principle of freedom of speech springs from the necessities of the program of self-government. It is a deduction from the basic American agreement that public issues shall be decided by universal suffrage.

. . . To be afraid of ideas, any idea, is to be unfit for self-government.[52]

Justice Brandeis, asserting that the greatest menace to freedom is an inert people, explained:

Those who won our independence believed that the final end of the State was to make men free to develop their facilities; and that in its government the deliberative forces should prevail over the arbitrary. They valued liberty both as an end and as a means. They believed liberty to be the secret of happiness and courage to be the secret of liberty. They believed that freedom to think as you will and to speak as you think are means indispensable to the discovery and spread of political truth; that without free speech and assembly discussion would be futile; that with them, discussion affords ordinarily adequate protection against the dissemination of noxious doctrine; . . . that public discussion is a political duty.[53]

Similar sentiments are encountered throughout recorded history. Herodotus admonished his fellow Greeks:

it is impossible, if no more than one opinion is uttered, to make choice of the best: a man is forced then to follow whatever advice may have been given him; but if opposite speeches are delivered, then choice can be exercised.[54]

The universal application of the elemental truth is noted by the twentieth-century Chinese philosopher Chung-Shu Lo:

In order to contribute fully to society, each individual should have the fullest degree of self-expression. Social progress depends on each individual's freedom of expression.[55]

The relationship is not a one-way affair. If free speech is a fundamental precondition of democracy, it is also in a democratic government that its most enduring protection is found. It is in this form of government that the strongest forces exist and, naturally, find expression among the intellectual as well as the popular sectors, to defend and guarantee the right of free expression. Thus, if free thought and expression are of critical importance to the continuing progress of man toward fair and just institutions, it is to democracy that we must look as the surest protection in the given human situation.

Exceptions to the above statements are frequently pointed out, and in the modern world the exceptions sometimes seem to predominate. They are most frequently encountered in situations of extreme economic discontent, where freedom and democracy appear to be of no avail. Or, where the literacy rate of the people is low, it is argued that free expression among them is meaningless since they do not have the tools with which to weigh what they are told. These arguments have been refuted in history. Injustice has been alleviated only when the condition of injustice has been made vivid to the dominant forces of the society. The full expression of all elements of the society are critical to that end.

Not only is freedom of expression a positive element in the progress of democratic societies; it has a negative aspect which is equally important to the survival of democracy. That element is the calling to account of public officials. Submitting persons exercising public office to the scrutiny of public opinion is one of the most effective instruments the people have to discourage abuse of public trust. This thought was present in the minds of the founding fathers of the United States:

> The last right we shall mention, regards the freedom of the press. The importance of this consists, besides the advancement of truth, science, morality and arts in general, in its diffusion of liberal sentiment on the administration of Government, its ready communication of thoughts between subjects and its consequential promotion of union among them, whereby oppressive officers are shamed or intimidated into more honorable and just modes of conducting affairs.[56]

Thus freedom of expression, permitting unfettered criticism of those in power, combined with the other elements of the system of democracy—competition for public power and removal from office—serves effectively to ensure the responsibility of those who must, in every society, be especially privileged to hold the reins of public power.

The rational basis of the concept was explained by Zechariah Chafee in his definitive work, *Free Speech in the United States:*

> Two different views of the relations of rulers and people were in conflict. According to one view, the rulers were the superiors of the people, and therefore must not be subjected to any censure that would tend to diminish their authority. The people can not make adverse criticism in newspapers or pamphlets, but only through their lawful representatives in the legislature, who might be petitioned in an orderly manner. According to the other view, the rulers were agents and servants of the people, who might therefore find fault with their servants and discuss questions of their punishment or dismissal, and of government policy.[57]

This is the heart of the problem, not only of free speech, but of all the rights of a self-governing society. To deny these rights, a government must set itself up as superior, in one manner or another, to the body politic. Apart from the philosophical implications of this orientation in relation to the over-all ignorance of all men concerning meaning and destiny, it is inimical to the basic precept of democracy that all men are free and entitled to equal opportunity. In democracy, the rulers are always the agents of a free citizenry. Free and equal men have the right to select the more capable and intelligent of their body to direct their affairs, but those so chosen gain thereby no prerogative to distort the thinking of the body politic by regulating and withholding its freedom to seek and discuss.

Democracy, nevertheless, has not been able to embrace the concept of complete freedom of expression without difficulty. Apart from the responsibility for abuses and errors committed in the exercise of the right of expression—a responsibility which has always been acknowledged—strong feelings have persisted throughout history that freedom of expression must also be subordinated to the necessity to protect the morals and order of the society and to the overriding interest of maintaining the peace and security of the state. This is on the theory that such limitations are essential to preserve the true freedoms of the majority. The French Declaration of the Rights of Man provides, in Article 10, that "No man ought to be molested on account of his opinions . . . provided his avowal of them does not disturb the public order established by the law." However, since then, as well as before, the patent lessons of history are that the state itself is the major threat to public order, safety, and freedom. But these lessons are lost when the majorities in a democracy become anxious for the protection of "their own interests."

The area of public safety and morals is one which has always been extremely sensitive for large groups within democratic societies. The justification for curtailing absolute freedom of speech relating to these areas is that it is necessary to maintain the morale and strength of the society by shielding it from supposed harmful and corrupting influences. In justifying these restrictions, a distinction is frequently drawn between a person in the capacity of a citizen participating in government and making political decisions, and a person in a private capacity, seeking his own advancement and advantage. This has been well expressed by Meiklejohn:

> If . . . the principle of the freedom of speech is derived, not from some supposed "Natural Right," but from the necessities of self-government by universal suffrage, there follows at once a very large limitation of the scope of the principle. The guarantee . . . is not, then, assured to all speaking. It is assured only to speech which bears, directly or indirectly, upon issues with which voters have to deal—only, therefore, to the consideration of matters of public interest. Private speech, or private

interest in speech, on the other hand, has no claim whatever to the protection of the First Amendment. That pronouncement remains forever confused and unintelligible unless we draw sharply and clearly the line which separates the public welfare of the community from the private good of any individual citizen or group of citizens.[58]

Differences in the object and nature of speech clearly exist, but the grave peril inherent in permitting these distinctions rests in the extraordinary powers it allocates over the liberty of expression to the person or persons who must make the distinctions and draw the lines. This is a substantive decision which is no longer in the hands of the people. Moreover, the people are unable to judge whether the distinctions are being wisely drawn, since they have not been fully and fairly exposed to the substance of what it is sought to exclude. Unless the privilege to draw these distinctions is employed with restraint, it presents an open-ended opportunity for abuse. Lurking behind these seemingly desirable measures are potentially convenient camouflages for those who would, wittingly or unwittingly, control the thought of the people and repress true self-government and self-reliance. These dangers are not as uncommon as may be thought. They are dramatized in the familiar story told by Tacitus that in ancient Rome it became law, after the time of Augustus, to permit the arrest of persons for obscenity. It soon became obscene, we are told, to criticize the Emperor. As Justice Black of the United States Supreme Court cogently observed, "It is not any trouble to establish a classification so that whatever it is that you do not want said is within that classification."[59]

Vesting the authority to draw these lines in the people's representatives, while the best solution to avoid abuses if these distinctions are insisted upon, is not without its perils. Justice Douglas warned that: "A great risk in any age is the tyranny of the majority. Freedom of expression is the weapon of the minority to win over the majority or to temper the policies of those in power."[60] The fundamental objective of the democratic system is to create and institutionalize a mechanism which will preserve the instruments of the system regardless of who or what faction of the society temporarily holds power. Where the spirit of self-government is firmly instilled in the society, perhaps it may then be argued that the power to exclude certain areas of speech from the right to free expression will be employed with good faith and good sense. But it is in these societies that the limitations are least needed. It is precisely in less politically stable societies, in which the spirit of democracy is not well established, and in which the limitations are most frequently invoked and most frequently abused, that the greatest vigilance is required.

The most delicate problem for a free society, in regard to the exercise of freedom of expression, is in the area of national security. Regardless of what dangers lurk in repressive measures, as a mask for those who would usurp power and repress democracy, strong emotions will undoubtedly continue to be mustered in support of these measures. This is natural. Speech is easy; it costs nothing. Although in itself it will not overthrow governments or cause disorders, it arouses the passions and stimulates the actions that do. The problem has a highly political nature, as was emphasized two centuries ago by Samuel Johnson:

> Every society has a right to preserve public peace and order, and therefore has a good right to prohibit the propagation of opinions which have a dangerous tendency. . . . He [the Sovereign] may be morally or theologically wrong in restraining the propagation of opinions which he thinks dangerous; but he is politically right.[61]

The right of the state or the existing order to defend itself was acknowledged, and simultaneously circumscribed, in the report of the UNESCO Committee on Human Rights in 1947: "Society is entitled to limit the exercise of these rights only in exceptional circumstances and only insofar as their exercise might endanger the existence of the society or the principles on which it is founded."[62] Although freedom is always exercised at some risk, control involves even greater perils, especially when that control has the possibility of becoming absolute and arbitrary. Restrictions on the freedom of expression, and curbs on the sources of public information have been principal elements in the temporary successes of totalitarian regimes.

The most important reason, however, signaling the threat to a free society by these measures lies in the inherent nature of that society. Its fundamental principle is freedom. Nonfreedom, whatever its reason, is inconsistent with its goal. This is not true of other societies. There is nothing inconsistent with efforts by Communism or fascism, or any other form of government to protect itself by limiting freedom, since it has not espoused this value to begin with. It is quite a different thing, however, when democracy protects itself by limiting freedom. It is like protecting your home from wear and tear by not using it and boarding it up. These restrictions, applied to the general population, seriously inhibit the ability of man to govern himself, regardless of whether those in power commit abuses. As John Stuart Mill characterized the effects:

> It is not the minds of heretics that are deteriorated most by the ban. . . . The greatest harm is done to those who are not heretics and whose whole mental development is cramped and their reason cowed by the fear of heresy. No man can be a great thinker who does not recognize that as a thinker it is his first duty to follow his intellect to whatever conclusions it may lead. Truth gains more even by the errors of one who, with due study and preparations thinks for himself than by the true opinions of those who hold them only because they do not suffer themselves to think.

The cardinal political issue in a democracy, as a self-governing society which relies upon the individual as the ultimate decision-maker, is to ensure that the individual is fully informed and aware of the true nature of the alternatives confronting his society. As expressed in 1937 by Chief Justice Charles Evans Hughes of the United States Supreme Court:

> The greater the importance of safeguarding the community from incitements to the overthrow of our institutions by force and violence, the more imperative is the need to preserve inviolate the constitutional rights of free speech, free press, and free assembly in order to maintain the opportunity for free political discussion to the end that government may be responsive to the will of the people and that changes, if desired, may be obtained by peaceful means. Therein lies the security of the Republic, the very foundation of constitutional government.[63]

Justice Oliver Wendell Holmes attempted to reconcile the contradictions in the problem in his formulation of the doctrine of "clear and present danger." He made the distinction that words can sometimes be more than words; they can be a form of action. To illustrate he observed that, "the most stringent protection of free speech would not protect a man in falsely shouting fire in a theatre and causing a panic," which would be tantamount to causing deaths. Justice Holmes injected the element of time as the critical factor determining when a government could or could not act to abridge free expression:

> when men have realized that time has upset many fighting faiths, they may come to believe even more than they believe the very foundation of their own conduct that the ultimate good desired is better reached by free trade in ideas—that the best test of truth is the power of thought to get itself accepted in the competition of the market; and that truth is the only ground upon which their wishes safely can be carried out. That, at any rate, is the theory of our Constitution. It is an

experiment, as all life is an experiment. Every year, if not every day, we have to wager our salvation upon some prophecy based on imperfect knowledge. While that experiment is part of our system I think we should be eternally vigilant against attempts to check the expression of opinions that we loathe and believe to be fraught with death, unless they so imminently threaten immediate interference with the lawful and pressing purposes of the law that an immediate check is required to save the country. . . . Only the emergency that makes it immediately dangerous to leave the correction of evil counsels to time warrants making any exception to the sweeping command, "Congress shall make no law . . . abridging the freedom of speech."[64]

Even broader license was requested in the United Nations in the discussions during the 1950's preceding the drafting of a convention on civil and political rights. Strong arguments were made for the legitimate circumscription of speech to prevent its exploitation for "war propaganda, incitement of hatred among peoples, racial discrimination and for the dissemination of slanderous rumors." Although ostensibly the motives are worthy, we quickly arrive at the question of who is to interpret these restrictions, and what protections are available to ensure that the interpreter does not abuse his authority but remains truly responsive to the necessities and sentiments of the prohibition. Although great reluctance was manifested in the United Nations discussions, the draft covenant finally included a prohibition of the advocacy of national, racial, or religious hostility where it "constitutes *an incitement* to hatred *and* violence."[65] As clearly specified, the advocacy must be an incitement, and that incitement cannot be to hatred alone, but must also involve violence.[66]

It is under any conditions a wide departure from the principle that there can be no crime of speech or thought, only crimes of actions. This doctrine was originally expressed by Thomas Jefferson, who said: "it is time enough for the rightful purposes of civil government for its office to interfere when principles break out into overt acts against peace and good order." More absolute than the limited restrictions permitted by Justice Holmes, Jefferson's formulation was grounded in the fact that democratic government was not an impotent, helpless creature simply waiting to be taken advantage of. As we shall discuss in Part Three, democratic government has numerous remedies against those who would abuse its privileges, and, in addition, an enduring strength rooted firmly in the natural expression of man's desires.

Wherever restrictions to free expression are permitted, two safeguards are imperative: the restrictions must be explicit, carefully defined, and clearly understood to preclude the indulgence in the indiscriminate use of this power by the state; and the state must be restrained from cutting off speech and discussion before it has occurred, and permitted to act only after an idea has been expressed and found to be harmful to the security and welfare of the society. This latter safeguard is what is commonly known as the prohibition of prior restraint.[67] The theory behind it is that punishment for abuses of the right to free speech can be applied only subsequent to the occurrence of the abuses. Besides the leverage which prior censorship has classically accorded to would-be usurpers of public power, the censor has an unavoidably demoralizing effect on the public. As graphically described by Milton in the *Areopagitica*, "there cannot be a more tedious and unpleasing journey-work" and the censor will inevitably be "either ignorant, imperious, and remiss, or basely pecuniary." A free people will not submit the fruit of their thought and labors to the approval of such censors.

The prohibition of prior restraint, however, has a very practical rationale which is equally applicable to the several forms of state action against the rights of man. It is based on the theory of probabilities. Should the state have the power to censor before an idea is known, it is more probable that such power could be abused than it is probable that an idea, no matter how dangerous and inflammatory, would endanger the state. Thus, democratic government must rely on laws of responsibility for abuses and must require that responsibility to be enforced in open court, with all possible safeguards and protection against arbitrary action of public power. Not only must the right to speak be free of previous restraint, it must also be free of the fear of arbitrary subsequent punishment, for the fear of an arbitrary, unjust penalty engenders an atmosphere which is equivalent to a previous restraint.

In modern times, a new dilemma has confronted those who seek to make the right to free expression an effective force in society. The limited number of airwaves, and the vast economic resources needed to reach an effective number of people through the media of mass communication are often in direct conflict with the concept of absolute freedom of expression. Unrestricted freedom of the few who possess adequate economic resources can easily become an instrument to manipulate the many, thereby rendering ineffectual the decision-making process essential to self-government. The threat here is not necessarily of direct propaganda, but of creating images and controlling access to ideas so that biases and predilections are embedded in the habits of the society, distorting its view of the truth and its receptivity to new directions. The entire structure and control of the communications media are sufficiently sensitive as instruments of self-government so that some methods must be devised to provide all segments of the population with access to them and an opportunity to publicize their ideas. In addition, some regulation through licensing is inevitable simply to allocate the limited air channels.

On the other hand, it is evident that no system of regulation can be permitted which would open the door to government control or influence over the dissemination of solely "desirable" ideas. The need to enable the body politic to be

exposed to all views, especially to some unpopular ideas
which may be relevant to the formulation of wise decisions in
a self-governing society, is a problem which will be increasingly urgent in modern democratic government.

The Right to the Protection of the Courts

Rights without remedies are worthless. All the rights imaginable—political, social, economic—are but empty shells unless, simultaneously, access to a free, independent institution
is available to grant remedies to enforce those rights. As we
have already observed, several constitutions and laws grant a
plethora of rights, but they are strange to the citizenry. No
matter how just the laws, if the administration of justice is
arbitrary, no man can be secure.

An impartial judicial authority safeguards those human
rights which, in turn, establish democracy. The committee
entrusted with the task of drafting the United Nations Draft
Covenant on Civil and Political Rights stated unequivocally
that "in the last analysis, the implementation of all the rights
in the covenant depended upon the proper administration of
justice."[68] That system of justice is, indeed, the bulwark of
democratic institutions. If the society is to be governed by
law, and immunize itself from the arbitrary discretion of any
one man or group of men, an independent judicial authority
must be able to ensure that the rule of law is maintained.

The functioning of that authority reinforces democratic
institutions in two equally important areas. First, should a
citizen's legitimate rights be interfered with or denied, the
citizen must have prompt, fair, and effective remedies available to summon his public officials to answer before the judiciary, which is empowered to command that they do or refrain
from doing specific acts which infringe those liberties An
efficient, responsive mechanism of this nature, ready to hear
the citizen's grievances, strengthens the confidence and self-
reliance which a citizen of a democracy must feel.

Second, the judiciary must protect individuals who are accused of crimes from unjust and arbitrary prosecution. The importance of these remedies to the establishment of the general security was emphasized by Montesquieu:

> Political liberty consists in security, or, at least in the opinion that we enjoy security. This security is never more dangerously attacked than in public or private accusations. It is therefore on the goodness of criminal laws that the liberty of the subject principally depends. . . . Liberty is in perfection when criminal laws derive each punishment from the particular nature of the crime. There are then no arbitrary decisions; the punishment does not flow from the capriciousness of the legislator, but from the very nature of the thing; and man uses no violence to man.[69]

This rein on the state's potentially all-encompassing power to prosecute and imprison criminals is particularly urgent if we accept those theories which sanction the subjection of human rights to restrictions for the general welfare and self-preservation of the society. An effective judiciary is essential to ensure that those limitations do not become license, for, with the overwhelming sovereign power of the state, such restrictions can be used to make democracy a theory, despotism a fact.

The responsibility of the state to establish a system of impartial justice, according the right to a hearing of accusations before "courts previously established in accordance with preexisting laws" is universally acknowledged.[70] Although frequently not incorporated into national constitutions by express reference as a "right" of man, it is generally considered to be "implicit."[71] Historically, it was among the original rights secured by the Magna Carta in its guarantee that no Englishman could be deprived of his personal freedom, life, or property except by judicial proceedings and the decision of his peers. It was underscored in the terse phrase: "To no one will we sell, to no one will we refuse or delay right or justice."[72]

Man has always regarded an impartial judiciary as indispensable to circumscribe the authority of those holding power, since monarchs, like authoritarians of all breeds, found it convenient to imprison opponents of their regimes. St. Augustine, too, in *The City of God,* proclaimed the essential nature of the fair administration of justice when he commented: "Justice being taken away, then, what are kingdoms but great robberies? For what are robberies themselves but little kingdoms?"[73]

Its role in a democracy is one of constant vigilance. Abuses emanate not only from the state, but from the people. John Stuart Mill felt impelled to caution against this in *On Liberty:*

> The will of the people . . . means the will of the most numerous or the most active *part* of the people; . . . the people, consequently, may desire to oppress a part of their number, and precautions are as much needed against this as against any other abuses of power. The limitation, therefore, of the power of government over individuals loses none of its importance when the holders of powers are regularly accountable to the community.

The protection is equally essential in shielding one group of society from another. Shakespeare's observation in *Measure for Measure* that "Liberty plucks justice by the nose" is not without cause. The principal function of the rights of the people is to ensure the minimum operating elements of the society which cannot be altered, regardless of who temporarily controls the public administration, and no matter how self-righteous they may consider themselves. Remedies must be available when rights are violated by any group, either systematically and deliberately, or in isolated instances. The right to those remedies is the protection of the democracy against its own moments of folly, and is one of the cardinal elements of a viable self-governing society.

The effective functioning of the judiciary is not easily attained. Unlike the other human rights which are in the nature of prohibitions, judicial protection requires the positive action of the state, and an elaborate and expensive organization. Furthermore, being an independent authority, and also because of the nature of its function—reconciling opposing interests—the judiciary is constantly subject to conflicting pressures and influences. Its balance and independence is delicate, and its effective operation depends more upon the moral fabric of the society than it does upon political theory.

An essential element in the effective functioning of the judiciary is that it attract the highest caliber of officials, and that it insist upon their adherence to the highest ethical standards. As for the judge, more often in his person and his independence than in the law itself, lies the fate of respect for human rights. Few other individuals in the society bear such great responsibility, with such immediate consequences, as does the judge, for his is often the sole decision in the interpretation of the facts or the law in cases which affect the economic livelihood or personal reputation of citizens.

As with all human rights, a fair and impartial judiciary is most easily secured under a democratic government in a free and open society. The sheer weight of the ultimate interests of the people (regardless of their economic and political persuasions) in preserving fair and impartial institutions is the only force which can, over a protracted period of time, hold these institutions in check and prevent their abuse. The equalization of power in a society is a force tending toward compromise and accommodation, and it is inevitably reflected strongly in the administration of justice.

THE RIGHT TO A FAIR TRIAL

If democracy is to afford its citizens judicial protection, to defend their rights when those rights are violated by persons clothed in the mantle of public power, the essence of such protection is the right to a fair trial. No punishments can be permitted except when imposed by competent authorities for offenses clearly defined by laws which existed before the claimed offense was committed, and after a fair and impartial hearing which affords the accused every opportunity to refute his accusers. If the government considers it necessary to deprive a man of his liberty by imprisonment, it must act to prove this necessity; it must gather evidence, present it to the courts in public, and substantiate its evidence. Only thus may a citizen rely on full protection against the arbitrary or oppressive action of his government. It is this reliance which enables him to function as an active, truth-seeking component of that democracy.

The ingredients of a fair trial are several, all derived from the principle that no man will be refused the opportunity to be heard, without delay or prejudice, before an unbiased judge. Often referred to as procedural due process of law, this concept has been summarized by the United States Supreme Court in the following language:

> The due process clause requires that every man should have the protection of his day in court, and the benefit of the general law, a law which hears before it condemns, which proceeds not arbitrarily or capriciously, but upon inquiry, and renders judgment only after trial, so that every citizen shall hold his life, liberty, property and immunities under the protection of the general rules which govern society.[74]

Although accused of being an unduly subjective standard, due process has certain specific elements that are identifiable as applied to judicial proceedings. The various draft international conventions have attempted to formulate universal applications.[75] In criminal proceedings, these include the right to be informed promptly of the nature and cause of the accusation, time to prepare a defense, the availability of legal counsel, the right to obtain witnesses, the privilege not to be required to testify against oneself, and the assistance of an interpreter where necessary. Moreover, punishment can be imposed only after the completion of the trial, according to the provisions of a clear and specific statute, and by a previously established court, not one created for the occasion. These are considered to be the minimum requirements of a mechanism which will effectively operate to discourage arbitrary abuse of public power.

The presumption of innocence, an intrinsic element of Western judicial protection, is rooted in a faith in the individual which must underlie any system of democracy. It is also a common-sense safeguard based on the fact that it is much more difficult to prove innocence than it is to prove guilt, and that the burden should be upon those who are trying to deny rights rather than those who seek to protect them.

Frequently it is urged that the right to a trial by jury is implicit in the right to a fair trial. In colonial times, when judges were appointed by a foreign aristocracy, this was indeed an important protection against the capriciousness of the court. Today, with the establishment of the judiciary as an independent branch of government, sometimes on a career basis, that rationale is no longer so applicable. The competence and impartiality of a trained judge, the recognition of sociological and psychological factors in criminal motivations, the increasing complexity of all types of litigation, and the crowded court dockets, all represent reasons for the diminishing need for such protection. On the other hand, the tolerance and understanding of a jury, which is able to mold and adjust rigid and impersonal laws by "interpreting facts," is often cited as an important element in favor of juries, in addition to its relative immunity to direct corrupt practices. Except where capital punishment is involved, however, the presence of a jury is not generally regarded as a critical element of the right to a fair trial.

The right to a trial in public has been more controversial.

It has always been considered vital to maintaining the actions of public authorities under the scrutiny of public opinion. It has been argued that the publicity of courtroom proceedings can frequently deny the accused a fair trial by creating an atmosphere whereby the issues are prejudged before all the parties have the opportunity to be heard, or where the social consequences will be equally severe as a result of the publicity, regardless of whether guilt or innocence is declared.

It is true that an orderly system of guarantees of human rights must distinguish between being tried *in* public and being tried *by* the public without the protection of legal procedure. The purpose of a public trial is to prevent secret trials, not to provide public amusement. But it is also true that once the right to limit public trial is sanctioned, it may be used "in the public interest," where the public interest is quite the contrary. It is a rare dictatorship which does not justify usurpation of power as a measure taken "in the public interest." Trials which are not subject to public review provide no security to the citizens of a democracy. Ultimately, they severely inhibit the functioning of the democracy, because the population will soon begin to wonder about the true motivations of closed proceedings. Suspicion and caution, instead of honesty and openness, will become the general rule, especially for those who oppose the policies of the regime in power. In the eighteenth century, Jeremy Bentham spoke forcefully against such proceedings:

> suppose the proceedings to be completely secret, and the court, on the occasion, to consist of no more than a single judge, that judge will be at once indolent and arbitrary; how corrupt so ever his inclination may be, it will find no check, at any rate no tolerably efficient check, to oppose it. Without publicity all other checks are insignificant; in comparison to publicity, all other checks are of small account. Recordation, appeal, whatever other institutions might present themselves in the charac-

ter of checks, will be found to operate rather as cloaks than checks; as cloaks in reality, as checks in appearance.[76]

The essence, however, of the right to a fair trial does not reside in the question of which legal system is applied, be it accusatorial or inquisitorial, or in rights to attorneys, or other legal rules which may help the accused. Fairness refers to the manner of application of impersonal rules, and its essence lies in the manner and the spirit in which the rules are administered. As was stated in a report of the International Commission of Jurists:

> the rights of the accused in criminal trials, however carefully elaborated, would be ineffective in practice unless they are supported by institutions, the spirit and tradition of which restrain and guide the exercise of the necessary discretion, whether in law or in practice, which belong in particular to prosecuting authorities and to the police.[77]

No one will maintain that democracy is the only sure and secure road to justice for mankind. The people as a whole, even though self-governing, are as apt to commit injustices as any despot. On a continuing basis, however, the concerted action of the people, the interacting forces generated in their free expression, the maintenance of checks over representatives and professional experts, directly or indirectly chosen by and responsible to them, are the most effective instruments man has devised to ensure a just administration of the law. The faith of the people in fair treatment by their institutions, which in essence is a faith in the ethical formation of their fellow men with whom they may be dealing on an impersonal basis, is essential to enable them to act and make decisions, freely and daringly, for themselves, and for their communities in a democracy. It is the operation of the judiciary which establishes the foundation of the faith of the citizen in the guarantees of democracy and human rights espoused by his society.

EX POST FACTO LAWS

An *ex post facto* law has been defined as "one which makes criminal and punishes an act which was done before the passage of the law and which was innocent when done."[78] It is also known as the principle of retroactivity, and has long been regarded as a bulwark against an unjust and oppressive public administration.[79] For this reason it is in democratic governments, where the representatives of the people must be overruled before this principle can be violated, that the right is most readily enforced. Should the power of the society rest with a small group of men who are not accountable to the people, their definition of crime can change without any check being available to preclude its arbitrary application.

Its relation to the practices of democracy lies not so much in its specific guarantee, although this is not to underestimate the importance of that guarantee, but in the atmosphere and feeling of security it fosters among its citizens. The psychological comfort derived from being able to rely on one's government for just treatment is fundamental to creating and maintaining a viable democratic state. As the International Commission of Jurists stated: "Retroactive legislation undermines the reasonable certainty of men in their daily activities which it is the object of a formal legal system to ensure."[80]

We have already discussed the crucial nature of the citizen's sense of security in a democratic state. The *ex post facto* prohibition contributes a large measure of that security, without which men cannot act freely to further their concepts of the best interests of the society.

The Right to Education

Thus far, the rights we have discussed in relation to the functioning of a democracy have been those identified as civil and political. Education is not a civil or political right, properly considered. It is so basic, however, to those rights and their effective operation that it is fraudulent to consider democratic government in today's world without it.

Because democracy depends on the understanding and participation of all citizens in its decisions, its decisions will be no better than allowed by the level of intelligence and perception of its individual citizens. In truth, representative democracy cannot long endure without education. Unless education develops parallel with the awakened consciousness of the people of their power within a democratic society, there is danger of creating more unrealistic expectations and dissatisfaction than a stable society may be able to bear. When Thomas Jefferson asserted that there was "no safe depository of the ultimate powers of society but the people themselves," he added, "if we think them not enlightened enough to exercise their control with a wholesome discretion, the remedy is not to take it from them, but to inform their discretion by education."

The natural resource of a democracy is human intelligence, fully cultivated and functioning. The belief that the most valuable natural resources are in our heads was the motivating conviction behind Chief Justice Warren's memorable opinion from the bench of the United States Supreme Court in 1954:

> Today, education is perhaps the most important function of state and local governments. Compulsory school attendance laws and great expenditures for education both demonstrate our recognition of the importance of education to our democratic society. It is required in the performance of our most basic public responsibilities. . . . It is the very foundation of good citizenship. In these days, it is doubtful that any child may reasonably be expected to succeed in life if he is denied the opportunity of an education.[81]

It was José do Manoel Bomfim, the turn-of-the-century Brazilian political theorist, who remarked that, for the development of men, all that was required was the right to make the curriculum in the schools; given that, he did not care who made the laws or the songs.[82]

Education is more than literacy. Literacy is but a tool with which to gain an education. To participate in government effectively a man must be able to understand the principles of his governmental system, he must be able to understand his own best interests, and view society and progress with some perspective. An education must convey this, together with a consciousness of the ultimate power and responsibility which is his in a system of self-government. A person may be granted all the civil and political rights imaginable, allowed to participate in his government by selecting his representatives, but unless he has been educated to understand these privileges his vote can be one of the greatest perils to democracy. This is especially true in today's world where all men wish to partake in a utopia immediately, while such a utopia can be created only by their own great efforts over a period of many years. The temptation of panacea vendors, in the midst of ignorance and poverty, of the demagogue adept at exploiting misery for personal gain, can be irresistible. Without education, the protections of democracy have meager attractions compared to the dream of rapid material benefits. More important, without an educated, enlightened constituency, representative government will not be able to govern, will vacillate before the pressing issues confronting the society, and will react with weakness and inaction instead of strength and determination. Representative democracy could survive all the external threats to its existence, yet be destroyed within itself if it fails to educate its citizens to participate and to understand the meaning of their participation.

We must not underestimate what is occurring in the ideological struggle engaging the world today. The fundamental premise upon which democracy is constructed is that "each man is the best judge of his own interest." In the complexity of that ideological struggle, however, this premise is totally inapplicable unless each of those men is able to understand the fundamental issues of that struggle. That issue is far more complex than simply a confrontation of the haves and the have-nots. It is a question of what type of institutions man will evolve to solve the question of the haves and the have-nots as the changing world transforms these groups. We must be aware that man is being educated to these issues, whether or not the society provides it for him in organized form. The absence of a formal education is as much an education as its presence. The most serious threat to a democracy could well be when it expands its political base rapidly and turns itself over to a majority who have gained nothing economically or socially from it, and to whom it has failed to convey an understanding of how to retain the ultimate power to improve the public welfare in a free society.

This threat will not go away. The pressures of the modern world demand that democracies turn themselves over to all of the people. Otherwise they will cease to exist and give way to repressive measures from one extreme or another. The passions which have been aroused are too intense to be ignored. The response of democracy must be to provide the people with an understanding of their own powers in a free, self-governing society; without this understanding they will succumb to those determined forces seeking to convince the people of the impotence of a democratic society. Education is more than the indispensable prerequisite, the *sine qua non,* if democratic institutions are to grow and mature; it is *the* urgent necessity if democracy is to survive. More than all the legal documents in the world, it will have the final impact on the future of democracy.

There is nothing new in the affirmation that the right to an education is as essential to political liberty as the very act of affixing one's mark to a ballot. John Stuart Mill declared: "Liberty . . . has no application to any state of things anterior to the time when mankind have become capable of being improved by free and equal discussion." To this he added that it is "almost a self-evident axiom that the state should require and compel the education up to a certain standard, of every human being who is born its citizen."[83] Centuries before, Epictetus had declared that: "The rulers of the state have said that only free men shall be educated; but Reason has said that only educated men shall be free." In Argentina, Domingo Sarmiento even used it as his definition for government, asserting, "To govern is to educate."[84]

Education is recognized as a basic human right in all national and international documents and pronouncements on human rights,[85] and has been stressed as "indispensable to the development of democracy."[86] In this sense it is impossible to overemphasize the necessity for democracy to exert extraordinary efforts for education. Democracy cannot be forced on a people, nor does it automatically educate its citizens to love its institutions. Democracy grows from the confidence and faith of a people in their own abilities, working together with their fellow citizens, to attend to their own needs and those of the community. It is a passion for self-government which must arise from people able and willing to feel that passion. It is therefore totally dependent upon an educated, informed electorate who have access to ideas and the opportunity to innovate and experiment with them. It is totally dependent upon people who have economic opportunity and do not spend their lifetimes in the endless, hopeless cycle of working constantly to produce enough to live so that they can go on working to go on living. Economic opportunity depends on the ability to see the opportunity and make a decision to work for it. The ability to see opportunity and to make decisions arises to a great measure from the education of the society. Only through education can a person learn his potential power in conducting his own affairs, and only in that manner can we arrive at the standard for a functioning democracy.

John Stuart Mill said of this standard: "the rights and interests of every or any person are only secure from being disregarded when the person interested is himself able, and habitually disposed, to stand up for them."

PART THREE

The Duties of Man and Limitations on Human Rights

Restrictions Due to Duties to One's Fellow Men

When asked by the United Nations Educational, Scientific, and Cultural Organization to contribute his ideas for a Universal Declaration of Human Rights, Mahatma Gandhi replied in these eloquent words:

> I learned from my illiterate but wise mother that all rights to be deserved and preserved come from duty well done. Thus, the very right to live accrues to us only when we do the duty of citizenship of the world. From this one fundamental statement, perhaps it is easy enough to define duties of Man and Woman and correlate every right to some corresponding duty to be first performed. Every other right can be shown to be a usurpation hardly worth fighting for.[1]

The concept of duty as an integral part of human rights pervades man's history and underlies the ethics and the evolution of modern civilizations. It was the meaning of the word "commandments" in the Ten Commandments; it was at the heart of the teachings of Jesus; it was implicit in Socrates' decision to obey the expressed will of the state and drink the hemlock.

The moderation of the rights of man by the duties of man, as thus expressed, is a broad and unwieldy concept and has been used as often to deprive men of legitimate rights as to protect them. In order to clarify their scope, these restrictions may be divided into three categories: (1) restrictions due to duties to one's fellow men, (2) restrictions due to duties to society, and (3) restrictions deriving from the necessity to preserve and maintain the security of the state.

Inherent in all human rights is the restriction that they not be used to injure other persons or to prevent others from enjoying their own rights. Mankind has always recognized this limitation as fundamental to the concept of human rights, having enshrined it in the so-called golden rule—"Do unto others as you would have others do unto you—" which is expressed in the code of ethics of every society and every religion. It was, perhaps, Gandhi's meaning when he spoke of citizenship of the world. It is the meaning of justice, and the impetus behind the concept of democracy. Not only is it essential to the preservation of that democracy, but emanating from the humanism of the eighteenth and nineteenth centuries, it was the rationale of democracy. All men owed respect to the rights of their fellow men, and those who were privileged to wield public power were no exception.

The foundation of a society adhering to the rule of law is a structure of rules defining the scope of one's duty to his fellow men. Thus, the positive law of the state, in the provisions of its penal and civil law, circumscribes these duties with penalties imposed by the state. Abuse of freedom of speech is penalized in libel and slander laws; unlawfully depriving another of his life or possessions subjects the offender to the sanctions of the penal codes; no one's liberty embraces the license to disregard his promises and commitments freely entered into with his fellow men. In a representative democracy, the nature and extent of these rules of the society are decided upon by representatives of the people and consented to by the people themselves in the exercise of their civil and political rights.

In spite of its embodiment in the general organization of the state, however, this respect is in many ways unenforceable by the state. It lies in the spirit of a people, in their sincere respect for their fellow citizens and in their desire to advance together with them in fair competition for a healthy society. Upon this respect for the human rights of one's fellow men all the other duties to society and the state are founded. It is inherent in the spirit of democracy and, upon it, democracy must rise or fall, succeed or fail.

Restrictions Due to Duties to Society as a Whole

Social responsibility must exist in a self-governing democratic society. Its absence imperils the very existence of democracy. Pieter Drost expressed the concept well:

> Too often democracy is identified with popular rights whilst real democracy is built on the political, economic and social responsibility of all citizens. Within the state as well as within the community of states, democratic society, which is founded on a respect for human rights of all persons and for the native rights of all peoples, can be secured and maintained only when the political, economic and social responsibilities corresponding to these rights are properly carried out.[2]

Thus, when we speak of respect for human rights, we imply not only the respect of the state for the rights of the citizen, but the respect of the citizen for the rights of the body of citizens. This respect cannot be restricted to respect for the rights of one person, or one class, or one group of persons. It must respect the rights of all groups, whether ethnic, religious, social, economic, political, or any other. The significance and preservation of democracy demands that it encompass the totality of the society.

The state is permitted certain powers of enforcement to ensure that the society maintains the order necessary to ensure respect for the rights of all. This power, generally known as the police power, has been characterized as an inherent attribute of civilized government and deemed "necessary in a democratic society," for the purpose of promoting the general order, health, safety, and public welfare of a society.[3]

If, in a democracy, a forum is to be assured to those who seek to influence the directions of the society, the police power is often essential to prevent the opposition of competing groups from infringing the rights of others or endangering local peace. It is especially pertinent in those areas where citizens seek change or hope to move the conscience of a society by actually disobeying, with peaceful, nonviolent methods, the established law of the society, which they consider unjust. Regardless of the merits of these demands, they must, as part of their protest and purpose to dramatize the injustice of the existing law, acknowledge the rights of the society to maintain order. If they fail in their purpose, they must submit to the laws of the society as they exist. The importance of this principle to a democracy was most dramatically related in the refusal of Socrates to accept the easy means provided for him to flee the laws which had condemned him unjustly. Refusing to conform to the substance of the law in his own life, he nevertheless acknowledged that he must accept the punishment that law meted out to those who failed to abide by it. He considered it equally important to his protest, which he sought to carry out within the framework of a democracy, to drink the hemlock and accept the consequences of his protest. While this was an extraordinary act carried out by an extraordinary man, it applies equally to all who would rebel against society, as pointed out by Albert Camus in his trenchant study *The Rebel*. When one willfully and knowingly chooses to destroy the institutions of the society in order to achieve his goals, he cannot then complain when that society reacts to his measures and seeks to destroy him in self-protection. Society, in this case, is acting according to precedent which he himself has accepted. Moreover, apart from ethical considerations, the practical consequence of retaliation must be expected.

Nevertheless, there are potential dangers to democracy in the concept of duty to the society and in the exercise of the police power which cannot be underestimated. The German scholar Kurt Riezler, who knew intimately the tragedy of Nazi Germany, warned against extending the concept of man's duties to this sphere. To him there could be but one duty: "Everyone's duty to recognize the human rights of his fellow citizen." He explained:

> If . . . these duties of man should be duties towards the "public welfare" of the "society" and the state, and rights are made conditional on the fulfillment of these duties, the duties will uproot the rights. The rights will wither away . . . [the] state can use the allegedly unfulfilled duties to shove aside the rights. . . . Any bill of rights that makes the rights conditional on duties towards society or the state, however strong its emphasis on human dignity, freedom, God, or whatever else, can be accepted by any totalitarian leader. He will enforce the duties while disregarding the rights.[4]

A similar admonition is contained in Article 4 of the French Declaration of the Rights of Man:

> Political liberty consists in the power of doing whatever does not injure another. The exercise of the natural rights of every man, has *no other limits* than those which are necessary to secure to every other man the free exercise of the same rights; and these limits are determinable only by the law [italics added].

The balance is a delicate one. On the one hand, a firm check on the power of the state must be maintained to ensure that the concept of public welfare is not exaggerated as a means of establishing a new oligarchy, or, as José María Luis Mora of Mexico stated more than a century ago, that the word "liberty" does not serve the destruction of the substance of liberty.[5] On the other hand, the survival of a democracy depends on the citizen's fulfillment of his obligations to the society as a whole. The state must be accorded certain police powers to ensure that these obligations are not abused by individual groups. The restraints on that police power must be found in the well-oiled functioning of the civil and political rights previously noted.

Social responsibility, however, is an essential concomitant to broad enjoyment of freedom and human rights. The danger always exists of overemphasizing rights before the concept of social responsibility is deeply imbedded in the personality of the society. Preying on man's aspirations for human rights, and using them as catchwords to lead unsuspecting peoples into new all-encompassing forms of economic and social bondage, has become a familiar sight in today's world. It can occur principally, however, where rights are extolled without the concept of social responsibilities.

Perhaps no matter what the theories, democracy will strike the balance between the power of the state and the rights of man only when the spirit of responsibility, understanding, and desire to maintain true democracy is so embedded in the population that the state's role in enforcing it becomes secondary, and applicable mainly to asocial personalities. This in turn can emerge only when justice exists within the state, which means the realization of full economic, social, and educational opportunities for all men.

Restrictions for the Security of the State

Perhaps the most widely known and most widely discussed grounds for restricting the exercise of human rights is the survival of the state itself.[6] Although this "right" to self-preservation in the current international order is more like an instinctive reaction which cannot be denied and will manifest itself whether or not anyone chooses to recognize it, the great dangers inherent in this "power" are everywhere evident. It provides the legal wedge which can and often has made human rights a fiction. In recognition of these perils the United Nations, in promulgating its Draft Covenant on Civil and Political Rights, stated that:

> It was . . . important that states parties *should not be left free to decide* for themselves when and how they would exercise emergency powers, because it was necessary to guard against states abusing their obligations under the Covenant. Reference was made to the history of the past epoch during which emergency powers had been invoked to suppress human rights and to set up dictatorial regimes [italics added].[7]

The potential pitfalls that lurk here are nowhere more in evidence than in the exploitation of the concept of "state of siege" made common in the states of the Western Hemisphere. No matter how perfect the theoretical statement of human rights contained in the constitution of a state, one provision within it contains the germ of destruction of all of those rights. This is the license to declare a state of siege. Originally designed for "grave dangers" to the state's survival, such as an invasion or actual "siege" by a foreign power, it was first formulated during the French Revolution. Its purpose, as then expounded by the French Assembly, was to serve as an institution distinct from a "state of war," in order to provide for more serious situations.[8] Today, it is applied equally to internal disturbances and threats of dangers to the security of the state. In the Americas, it has been characterized as the most abused of all Latin American Constitutional provisions,[9] which is easily verifiable from the fact that the decade 1950–60 saw it invoked more than a hundred times in Latin America, although the decade brought no wars or invasions, and hardly any threats of invasion. The same decade, however, saw more than a dozen dictators come and go or remain in power.

The state of siege, which for reasons of the security of the state, licenses "the suspension in all the national territory . . . [of] the guarantees established in the constitution" poses a twofold peril to the survival of democracy. Its constant threat to derogate those rights essential to the functioning of a democracy effectively dampens the atmosphere of security which must be firmly established if men are to act freely and honestly. It also has immediate effects on the checks and balances and the separation of powers upon which the maintenance of democratic institutions depends. Under the state of siege the discretionary powers of the executive are increased, in some cases to the extent that the power of the legislature is completely annulled.[10] If the executive power alone has the authority to declare and terminate the emergency by which the separation of powers is suspended, there is obviously no constitutional means to prevent wholesale abuse. History, in fact, as pointed out in the extensive study by the Inter-American Commission on Human Rights, provides ample testimony to the fact that the state of siege is most often invoked on the pretext of a threat to the state which in reality amounts to no more than a challenge to the personal power of those in office.[11]

The ever-present danger of using an institution, such as the state of siege, as a repressive measure for reactionary purposes,[12] well dramatizes the dangers inherent in granting the society the right to limit human rights for its self-preservation. Although its use is obviously a result, rather than a cause of political instability, and its elimination or restriction will not deter those who are intent on perpetrating the abuses which are presently committed under its name, we can, at least, make it impossible for usurpers of public power to drape their actions with a mantle of legality in its name. If antidemocratic actions are to be taken, the least we can do is label them clearly and not allow them to parade as temporary measures "to preserve and maintain the democratic institutions." By defining a legal democratic regime more carefully, and outlining as precisely as possible those situations in which such measures are permissible, perhaps we shall be able to eliminate this pernicious type of masquerade.

The most critical and urgent problem for democracy today, however, arises from the existence of opponents to this system of government who seek to take advantage of the privileges accorded by a free society to destroy that freedom and democracy. This engenders harsh reactions from many citizens who have a deep regard for free institutions. The U.S. legal philosopher Max Radin observed that: "There is a strong tendency in time of war for many sober citizens to demand a severer, harsher, more drastic and more expeditious enforcement of all types of police regulations than they would endure in time of peace."[13] This applies not only in time of war. The threat of subversion, the actions of those who would destroy the society at any cost, cause a constant outcry for extreme measures to combat the threat. Alexander Hamilton touched on the problem in *The Federalist:* "Safety from external danger is the most powerful director of national conduct. Even the ardent lover of liberty will, after a time, give way to its dictates. . . . To be more safe, they at length become willing to run the risk of being less free."[14] The intensity of the fears and emotions has even caused responsible international organizations to succumb to making statements such as this: "It can be said that the elimination of constitutional obstacles by means of the suspension of individual guarantees constitutes an indispensable condition for the adoption of legislative measures for defense."[15] When those organizations recommend for adoption the very methods employed by totalitarian governments to achieve their ends,[16] the seriousness of the threat to freedom, from friend and foe alike, becomes evident.

The reconciliation of these apparent opposites is a critical one. Limiting freedom to protect security, or, conversely, to maintain freedom at the risk of security, are both perilous alternatives. Although a strong case can readily be made for the essential function of some of these restrictions, the question really resolves itself into one of proportion. If we are fully aware of what we are doing, and remain cognizant of the dangers inherent in our actions—using good sense and maintaining vigilance against abuse, and, most important, keeping channels open by which we can correct our mistakes when we find them to be such—then we may be able to survive some of these limitations. The risks, however, rise in direct proportion to the lack of maturity of the democracy. In immature societies, these measures frequently lead to a usurpation of power and a regime as destructive of democracy and freedom as the one which it sought to eliminate. The peril of destroying the state by the very measures we employ to protect it, of creating precedents which will enable those who have no respect for human rights to disregard those rights, becomes increasingly greater in those very countries where popular discontent is high because the government has not fulfilled its proper functions in the past.

It is well to recall that the alternative to these extreme measures is not impotence. A democracy is not without strong powers to combat those who plot against it. Aside from the normal exercise of the police power discussed above, there are express laws against overt acts of violence, secreting of arms, destruction of public and private property, treason and conspiracy. The one measure, however, that a democracy insists upon in these cases is a procedural safeguard—the necessity of proving its charges in open court. The preservation of this protection, in the interests of all the citizens of the society, was discussed in Part Two. Those principles are most critical in cases of national emergency, at which time the true mettle of a democracy is put to the test.

The use of emergency powers in the United States affords an interesting illustration of the importance of limiting their scope. Those powers are carefully circumscribed in the Constitution, which provides only for the suspension of the right of habeas corpus, and then solely "when in cases of rebellion or invasion the public safety may require it." Allowable restrictions of other rights have been demarcated in the opinions of the Supreme Court by what is called the doctrine of "clear and present danger," formulated by the Supreme Court in these words: "Any attempt to restrict those liberties must be justified by clear public interests threatened not doubtfully or remotely, but by clear and present danger."[17] In the interpretation of this ruling the Court has held that thought and advocacy of ideas which threaten the security of the state can never be a danger of such a nature to be penalized by the state; only overt action toward the forcible overthrow of the established government can be penalized by the full force of state power. In fact, the United States has passed through two World Wars with minimal restrictions on the personal liberties of its citizens, especially in comparison to the measures imposed in states of siege in other countries.

The analysis of emergency powers in the United States, in relation to the liberties guaranteed by the Constitution, was commented upon by Supreme Court Justice David Davis following the Civil War:

> No doctrine, involving more pernicious consequences, was ever invented by the wit of man than that any of its [the Constitution's] provisions can be suspended during any of the great exigencies of government. Such a doctrine leads directly to anarchy or despotism, but the theory of necessity on which it is based is false; for the government, within the Constitution, has all the powers granted to it which are necessary to preserve its existence. . . . This nation . . . cannot always remain at peace. . . . Wicked men, ambitious of power, with hatred of liberty and contempt of law, may fill the place once occupied

by Washington and Lincoln; and if this right is conceded, and the calamities of war again befall us, the dangers to human liberty are frightful to contemplate. If our fathers had failed to provide for just such a contingency, they would have been false to the trust reposed in them. For this, and other equally weighty reasons, they secured the inheritance they had fought to maintain, by incorporating in a writing the safeguards which time had proved were essential to its preservation.[18]

Thus, it was concluded that even though habeas corpus could be suspended in time of national emergency, it was only because it might be impossible to provide immediate public investigation. But no conviction or punishment could be effected without a normal trial by pre-established civil courts, according to law. It is made clear that it is the civilian judiciary which has the ultimate voice when the lawfulness of military actions is questioned regarding infringements of the liberties of citizens.[19] So long as the regular courts are open and unobstructed by direct military action, neither the executive nor the legislative branch can abrogate its jurisdiction over the protection of the rights of the people, which rights are embodied in the Constitution in absolute terms: "Congress shall make *no* law. . . ."

In the last analysis, democracy must be no less insistent on maintaining its principles than other systems are in maintaining theirs. Any Communist will affirm that one cannot achieve Communism by surrendering or compromising any of the principles of Communism. No dictator will relax his grip or compromise the principles of his power to make his regime more palatable. Although the analogy is difficult for democracy, since it is the antithesis of these regimes, in the long run democracy will not be secure except by firm faith in and adherence to the principles of democratic government. If it surrenders those principles for the ostensible purpose of meeting a threat to its survival, it no longer has anything unique to protect. Democracy has an inner strength, based on man's unquenchable spirit and desire for self-expression. Combined with the rule of law and normal protections against its enemies, this spirit will, if it remains true to its principles, capture the imagination of all men and ultimately triumph, for human rights and self-government are the cause of mankind.

PART FOUR

The Road Ahead— And the Role of International Organization

In relation to representative democracy, human rights are more than ideal formulations of some utopian goal. They are the integral mechanism of democracy, implicit in the very nature of democracy It is not a theoretical question of good or bad, necessary or supplemental. Whatever else may be said of them, the rights are pragmatic, practical elements of representative democracy, without which it cannot function.

Conversely, the only genuine guarantee that those human rights will be observed is to place the ultimate control of the machinery of government in the hands of the people themselves. The human situation will allow no one man or group of men to claim a monopoly of knowledge or, on the basis of that knowledge, a monopoly of power. Abuse would be inevitable. Unfettered participation by the people in the control of their institutions, whether it be in the local community or in national programs, is the only enduring way of providing for and ensuring fairness and just application to the needs of all.

Placing the machinery of government in the ultimate control of the people to maintain the supremacy of the will of the people does not mean, however, that the will of the people is absolute unto itself and that democratic government is nothing more than the mechanical determination and carrying out of the popular will. Were this all that is involved, a Univac would make the best legislature, with an IBM design serving as executive. The popular will is not infallible and can commit the same abuses as any other despot. For this reason it must, in a true democracy, remain subject to certain principles designed to ensure the continued functioning of the democracy. These principles are those human rights, enumerated in the constitutional guarantees and in the international declarations, which set forth the framework, or the ground rules, if you will, of a viable democracy. While it may seem contradictory to assert that the registering of the will of the people must be limited, and the objection may be raised that this injects elements of "natural law," it is not, in fact, contradictory. No proponent of natural law throughout its philosophical development ever formulated a "Bill of Rights" or a "Declaration of Human Rights." These limits are strictly a reasonable and pragmatic interpretation of those principles necessary to ensure the faithful and continued functioning of an orderly and just society, which reflects the wishes of the governed in its principal decisions and remains sufficiently flexible to accommodate to changing needs. It implies nothing about social or economic theory, whose content may change radically over the years. It says only that, whatever economic or social theory is preferred, the way must be left open to change it in case of error or of a shift in preference. It recognizes that not even majorities are infallible and defines the scope of their action within these functional limits.

It is obvious that, given the best of conditions for a democracy, the power wielded by the people can be abused. Where economic benefits are restricted to a small minority, the impatience of the people may demand extreme measures. The power of the demagogue, operating within the context of the democracy, is always a threat. It often seems difficult and callous to tell those who consider themselves deprived that the abuses may be greater under other systems. Yet history has irrefutably proved that where the people choose to forgo checks and controls over their rulers, for the sake of rapid remedies, their situation does not improve; the same hardships inevitably remain, subject to the will of new masters.

While it is the surest means of safeguarding the rights of all people, the democratic process is slow. Moreover, equal participation of all people in democratic institutions cannot be achieved overnight. To participate effectively, people must be aware of their institutions and conscious of the ultimate power and responsibility which are theirs. Given the patrimonial social structures existing in many parts of the world, a free society can be realized only by an intensive and thoughtful program of education. Almost more important than teaching reading and writing, this education must teach the principles of the power and responsibilities of a free society.

The judgment of the people must be as informed and as intelligent as it is within our limited powers to achieve if they are to participate effectively in the inquiry and discussion which is a prelude to the selection of those citizens who will be entrusted with public power. An understanding of the political issues is essential if there is to be assurance that the decision of the majority will effect a reasonable adjustment of the conflicting interests of the society.

If men are to overcome indolent habits of the past, and democracy is to be made to function, participation in democratic government must be made more real to the people. In all governments of the Western world today the very size of government tends to prevent people from identifying with its goals. The ballot is not always sufficient to close the gap. The smaller units of government, on the local level, must be made more personal and the counsel of the people solicited at every turn. In addition, institutions must be devised and encouraged which will foster participation in community activities, to accomplish social purposes without state intervention. Only thus will people come to feel the responsibilities of their government and to understand the problems of progress. This is vital to the furtherance of respect for human rights, because only among people truly convinced of their role and responsibilities can representative democracy succeed in securing the basic human rights for all men.

Ultimately, the participation of all men in their governments and in assuring respect for human rights is closely linked to the peace of the world. The relationship was forcefully emphasized in 1958 by Ambassador Julio A. Lacarte of Uruguay:

> Violations of liberty mean the existence of abusive power, and this, in turn, means the breakdown, not of the moral law only, but of the legal standards. And on the human level, from such violations spring violence, oppressions, and hatred, and on the international level, threats to peace and to the rule governing harmonious relationships among nations.[1]

This current of thought has predominated in international affairs in this century since the idea of self-determination of peoples and Woodrow Wilson's insistence upon popular government shaped the Versailles Treaty negotiations after World War I. Faced with the real aspiration of the people for more liberty, and a greater voice in the conduct of their affairs, any government which tends to deny or repress those aspirations promotes internal dissensions and tensions, and spawns dissident groups which feel compelled to resort to violent means to attain their goals. This in turn forces those governments to divert even more of their resources from the constructive programs of improving the social and economic conditions of their people. The environment becomes an incubator for the enemies of democracy, who proclaim their exclusive ability to satisfy economic and social aspirations; as their power becomes more evident, the chances of international conflagrations multiply as the powerful democracies are confronted with a more intransigent situation.

Those nations which deny human rights to their peoples are not operating in isolation; they are shaping the history of the world just as surely as those nations which are seeking to develop true democracy. Repression affects the outlook for the development of free institutions everywhere. The longer this continues, the less time remains for true democratic institutions to take root. The "protection" of one people today by limiting their freedom of expression may mean the enslavement in another guise of other peoples tomorrow. There is no way of knowing how or when it will strike, but the threat is ominous.

Under traditional international law, it has been held that the choice of whether to recognize individual human rights, or even to practice representative democracy, resides with each individual state. Within the present legal structure of the inter-American system, for example, the Inter-American Juridical Committee has stated that no basis can be found for collective action to defend or restore democracy in any of the American states,[2] citing Article 15 of the Charter of the Organization of American States, which provides that "No State or group of States has the right to intervene, directly or indirectly, for any reason whatever, in the internal or external affairs of any other State. . . ."

Numerous states, sensitive to the abuses of past history, seek, at almost any cost, to preserve the principles of nonintervention and self-determination as essential to the maintenance of national identity. It is patent, however, that if collective action is unavailable to preserve democratic institutions, and states remain free to violate human rights within their own borders, no international declarations or conventions can be meaningful. Worse, the principle of nonintervention is often self-defeating. Those states which perpetrate the most flagrant abuses of democracy and human rights are those who most frequently claim the protection of the international community from "intervention" when the wrath of their citizens and those of neighboring states seeks violent remedies to uproot the evil. The recent cases of Cuba and Haiti in the Organization of American States and of South Africa and Hungary in the U.N. dramatize the critical deficiency in the present practices of international organization. The abuses of those governments—their internal disregard for human rights —were beyond the reach of any international organization.

Unquestionably, grave problems arise when we attempt to give powers to an international organization over matters which, historically and traditionally, have been solely within the domestic jurisdiction. The abuses of the past, similar to the abuses we have referred to in citing the need for democracy, are real. The warning of the Inter-American Juridical Committee of a "crusade of the democracies," likened to the old Holy Alliance, is not to be lightly dismissed.[3] On the other hand, there is a basis for action which is not entirely open to the abuses many fear. As was stated in 1962, at the Symposium on Representative Democracy, held in the Dominican Republic:

> [Under the principle of nonintervention] any action by a State or a group of States that involves undue interference in the internal affairs or interests of another State or group of States, whether requested or permitted by the government or governments concerned, shall be declared illegal. In that sense, the idea of nonintervention is a projection into the sphere of international relations of the ideas of freedom and equality in relations between individuals in a given State.
>
> On the basis of that interpretation of the principle, the fol-

lowing actions cannot be described as intervention: examination of the conduct of governments, carried out either privately or publicly by individuals from other States; acts of international cooperation that are accepted by a State and are inspired by a desire to achieve the principles and goals of the regional organization; actions by the authorities of the regional organization in fulfillment of international standards freely consented to by the State towards which they are directed.[4]

When the rights of citizens within a nation are abused, the manner in which the domestic law of that nation functions is to submit them to a superior power which derives its authority from the implied prior consent of those who are affected by its actions. The same principle is applicable to the international scene. In this stage of history, the consent of a nation obviously must be expressed. No one will venture to "imply" the acquiescence of a state for any realistic purpose. But on some occasions such consent is given, as it is with adherence to an instrument such as the Charter of the Organization of American States, which, in Article 5, paragraph d, states: "The solidarity of the American States and the high aims which are sought through it require the political organization of those States on the basis of the *effective exercise* of representative democracy" (italics added). When such a statement is agreed to and ratified by the legislature of a nation, it should be considered on its face, and international agencies ought, at least, to resolve doubts in favor of the literal meaning of the words.

This will not be easy to achieve. States do not readily sign agreements which derogate some of their historic sovereignty. Agreements involving human rights and democracy receive many accolades and much approval which do not constitute legal commitments. This is clearly evident when it is observed that in the period when some of the most high-sounding resolutions on human rights were approved by the inter-American system, many of the Latin American states were subjected to authoritarian rule, and in some, fundamental human rights were a mockery. Indeed, in 1948, when the American Declaration of the Rights and Duties of Man was adopted, almost half of the American states had not completely rid themselves of authoritarian governments. The United Nations' record is not very different. The fact that a country subscribes to the Universal Declaration of Human Rights holds no guarantee of its observance.

This must be changed. The great challenge of our day is to gain time for the spirit of democracy to grow. It is obvious that the nations of the hemisphere must join together and help one another to achieve true free institutions. If international intervention is feared, then we must devise specific international standards which preclude arbitrary interference and intervention to take measures to further these rights. The difficulty of the task must not deter us. The guideposts to our future path have been set; they await only our action.

In the last analysis, only the spirit and true exercise of democracy can guarantee enduring respect for human rights. The first step toward this end is to define, as clearly as possible, those human rights and their relationship to democracy, a step toward which it is hoped that this study will make a modest contribution.

Appendix

Appendix

HUMAN RIGHTS AND REPRESENTATIVE DEMOCRACY*

The purpose of this short commentary is to set forth the reasons why the fundamental human rights contained in the American Declaration of the Rights and Duties of Man are essential to democracy, and conversely, why the democratic form of government is indispensable to ensure the observance of those fundamental rights.

Many declarations of the American states enunciate the essential rights of man. In the Charter of the Organization of American States, Article 5(j), the American states proclaim "the fundamental rights of the individual without distinction as to race, nationality, creed or sex." The same Charter, in Article 5(d), provides that "the solidarity of the American states and the high aims which are sought through it require the political organization of those States on the basis of the effective exercise of representative democracy." Notwithstanding these affirmations, a great need remains to relate in a concise form the reasons why human rights and representative democracy are important to each other, indeed, are inseparable.

The need for such a statement is clear. To a large segment of humanity in the modern world these concepts, accepted as unquestioned principles in many areas, have no meaningful content. Leaders of people subjected to totalitarian regimes

* This document, published in April, 1965, was prepared at the direction of the Inter-American Commission on Human Rights by its Secretariat. It is based upon the text of the "Second Report on the Relationship Between Human Rights and Representative Democracy," by Dr. Durward V. Sandifer, Member of the Commission.

affirm that civil and political rights are a fiction and that the most important rights of man are the economic rights.

Without deprecating these economic rights, it seems necessary to re-emphasize that far from being secondary rights, the civil and political rights are the forerunners of the economic and social rights; that democratic governments must be rooted in a firm recognition of these rights and liberties; and that without the civil and political rights, all men are dependent on the volatile benevolence of those persons who seize power, no matter how socially conscious their government pretends to be.

In explaining these rights, the commentary accepts several underlying premises. It is grounded in the belief that governments exist for the purpose of promoting the welfare and human dignity of each member of society. It has confidence that individual men have it within their power to achieve happiness for themselves and their posterity, working together in the common interest as they themselves freely understand and conceive that interest. It is convinced that the government and law must be instruments to serve the people and not the people the servant of the government and the law.

The insistent demands for social and economic justice heard in today's world have given rise to new and strenuous efforts to improve the welfare of all people. The objective and purpose of those efforts, however, should never be lost from sight. That purpose is to attain a full and happy life in an atmosphere of freedom and security for all men—that is the imperative of human rights.

With that purpose in mind, new urgency attaches to the need for strict observance of civil and political rights which alone can ensure that government remains responsive to the needs of the people. Understanding this, and realizing that the principal aim of representative democracy is to provide the mechanism for orderly change of men's social and economic situation and continual accommodation to mankind's emerging needs, the following commentaries on the civil and political rights which are essential to the effective functioning of representative democracy have been formulated.

I. THE RIGHT OF THE INDIVIDUAL TO LIFE, LIBERTY AND THE SECURITY OF HIS PERSON constitutes the purpose for which governments are instituted and the foundation upon which representative democracy must rest.

Only in an atmosphere of security for life and liberty can men act and vote in their own best interests and in that of society. While the rule of law is the prerequisite to ensure that the life, liberty and security of the people is not abused, representative democracy, as the expressed sovereign will of the people, is the only form of government which can truly ensure that the law will observe and continue to fulfill its designated function.

II. THE RIGHT TO DUE PROCESS OF LAW secures to the citizen those rights which belong to him under the law in a representative democracy.

No law or actions of the state can deprive any person of life or liberty without following lawful procedures and affording the individual every possible protection against arbitrary and unjust acts committed by the authorities. The respect for this right is basic to the functioning of a representative democracy in that it enables the citizen to guide his conduct, to weigh and discuss the functioning of his government and the directions of his society without fear. The full confidence of the people in this right can be achieved only where governmental authority is clearly circumscribed by rules of law which preclude the arbitrary exercise of power and afford the citizen the opportunity to contest the validity of measures taken against him.

III. THE RIGHT TO FREEDOM FROM ARBITRARY ARREST, TO THE INVIOLABILITY OF THE HOME AND TO PRIVACY guarantees to every citizen the opportunity to act in freedom from fear.

The observance of these rights prevents the invasion of a citizen's privacy without full legal safeguards, both in his home and in communication. These rights are most secure in a representative democracy where due process of law is guaranteed, and where those men who are entrusted with public responsibility are held to account to the people.

IV. THE RIGHT TO THE PROTECTION OF THE COURTS underlies the rule of law upon which depends the enjoyment of all other rights.

Human rights are devoid of substance unless the people can appeal to a free, independent authority providing adequate and effective remedies to enforce those rights. A citizen must be secure in the knowledge that he will be accorded a fair and impartial hearing which will afford him full protection against arbitrary action by his government. The protection of human rights by a fair and impartial judiciary preserves the integrity of representative democracy.

V. THE RIGHT TO EQUAL PROTECTION BEFORE THE LAW stands as the inalienable obligation of representative democracy to every citizen.

All citizens must be treated as equal before the law without discrimination for race, creed, sex, language, political conviction or social condition. Discrimination can only be eliminated where absolute power does not rest in the hands of one man or a small group of men. This right can be secure only under a representative democracy where every citizen is able to act directly and in combination with other citizens to insist on an equal share in the benefits of the society without having to rely on the whim or benevolence of any particular person or group.

VI. THE RIGHT TO PARTICIPATE IN FREE ELECTIONS is the cornerstone of responsible representative democracy.

One of the principal achievements of mankind is to provide for orderly changes in government according to the true will of the people under a system of representative democracy which relies on the will of the people as the source of power. The participation of the people in the choice of their leaders through secret, honest, periodic and free elections guarantees such orderly change and averts the destruction and violence which ensue when men succumb to the temptation of power. Any derogation from this principle, under whatever pretext, is a deception which, persisting, means the enslavement of the people and the destruction of their rights.

VII. THE RIGHT TO FREEDOM OF MOVEMENT is an integral part of the individual liberty necessary to the effective functioning of representative democracy.

The right to move about freely within and without the country must be permitted and guaranteed by those who have the responsibility of power within a representative democracy, without any limitations other than that provided by due process of law.

The free exercise of this right fosters the confidence of the citizen in the government, increases his understanding of national problems, and develops his civic consciousness.

VIII. THE RIGHT TO FREEDOM OF EXPRESSION, INFORMATION AND INVESTIGATION assures to every citizen the privilege of criticism, experimentation, communication and access to sources of information and investigation. The effective guarantee of these liberties enables representative democracy to develop the fair and just institutions essential to the general welfare.

Without free diffusion of thought and adequate access to sources of information, both national and foreign, public opinion, which alone guarantees the effectiveness of representative democracy, cannot be wisely or well developed. This right cannot be denied to the people, not even by those.citizens selected and entrusted as their representatives.

IX. The Right to Peaceful Assembly, to Associate with Others and to Petition forges a representative democracy responsive to the needs and the will of the people.

To participate effectively in representative democracy a citizen must be able to bring his thoughts and desires to the attention of the government, for which purpose his right to join with other citizens cannot be denied. To stifle or attempt to control the right of the citizen to associate freely with whom he chooses or to petition for a redress of grievances is to suppress the source of ideas and actions of the very people to be governed. This right is one of the basic attributes of representative democracy which relies on the thoughts and actions of all its citizens to determine its course of action, and which neither fears nor suffers but rather seeks and benefits from the associations and public airing of grievances.

X. The Right to an Education assures to every citizen a share in the benefits of science and culture to the extent that it is possible for a government to do so.

This right, which belongs to every human being, is the indispensable prerequisite to the growth and maturity of democratic institutions. The higher the level of education of its citizens, the more effective and dynamic will be the democracy. The basic natural resource of democracy is human intelligence, fully cultivated by an education which empowers it to comprehend its rights and duties and to participate effectively in the development of a democratic society.

XI. The Exercise of These Rights with full understanding of the duties and responsibilities they imply assures the strength of the system of representative democracy.

Rights and duties are correlative, and the principal objective of government is to harmonize the rights of one citizen with those of others. Each citizen, as a member of a free and democratic society, should be prepared to cooperate in the protection of the rights of his fellow citizens.

Notes

Notes

PART ONE: THE PROBLEM

1. Francisco Bilbao, "Sociabilidad Chilena," in *Obras* (Santiago de Chile, 1865), I, 37–38. Translation in William Rex Crawford, *A Century of Latin-American Thought* (rev. ed.; Cambridge, Mass.: Harvard University Press, 1961), p. 70.

2. Albert Camus, *Resistance, Rebellion, and Death*, trans. Justin O'Brien (New York: Alfred A. Knopf, 1961), p. 103.

3. William Graham Sumner, *Folkways* (rev. ed.; New York: Blaisdell, 1965), sects. 56 and 70.

4. Acts 25:16.

5. Pieter N. Drost, *Human Rights as Legal Rights* (Leiden: A. W. Sijthoff, 1951), p. 251.

6. Learned Hand, "The Spirit of Liberty," in *The Spirit of Liberty*, ed. Irving Dilliard (New York: Alfred A. Knopf, 1953), p. 190.

7. From Juan Bautista Alberdi, "Fragmento preliminar al estudio del derecho," in *Obras completas*, I, 112–13. Translation in Crawford, *op. cit.*, p. 28.

8. For a review of the principles of this early political thought, see Hersch Lauterpacht, *International Law and Human Rights* (New York: Frederick A. Praeger, 1950), pp. 83–84.

9. Adolf A. Berle, *Latin America: Diplomacy and Reality* (New York: Harper & Row, 1962), pp. 22–23.

10. Resolutions X and XI, Fourth Meeting of Consultation of Ministers of Foreign Affairs, Washington, D.C., 1951. Reaffirmed, Seventh Meeting of Consultation of Ministers of Foreign Affairs, San José, 1960, Resolution VII.

11. UNESCO, *Human Rights, Comments and Interpretations* (New York: Columbia University Press, 1949), p. 263.

12. Alexander Meiklejohn, *Free Speech and Its Relation to Self-Government* (New York: Harper & Bros., 1948), p. 85.

13. Foreign Minister Raúl Roa of Cuba, speech before the Council of the Organization of American States, in Pan American Union, *Minutes*

of the Meeting of the Council of the OAS, Washington, D.C., March 18, 1959.

14. Abraham Lincoln, Address at Sanitary Fair, Baltimore, Md., April 18, 1864, in *Collected Works of Abraham Lincoln* (New Brunswick, N.J.: Rutgers University Press, 1953), VII, 301–2.

15. Charles de Secondat, Baron de Montesquieu, *The Spirit of the Laws,* trans. Thomas Nugent (New York: Hafner, 1949), I, 8.

16. No precise figures are available for the initial elections, but as late as 1824 the electorate consisted of 350,000 persons out of a total population of more than 10 million. See Samuel Eliot Morison and Henry Steele Commager, *The Growth of the American Republic* (New York: Oxford University Press, 1955), I, 790. See also *The World Almanac,* 1962, p. 418.

17. Camus, *op. cit.,* p. 161.

18. Montesquieu, *op. cit.,* p. 8.

19. Cited in Crawford, *op. cit.,* p. 97.

20. *Corpus Juris Secundum,* XVI, 974.

21. G. W. F. Hegel, "The Philosophy of Right," sec. 154.

22. *Corpus Juris Secundum,* XVI, 974.

23. Hans Kelsen, *What is Justice?* (Los Angeles: University of California Press, 1960), p. 10.

24. Camus, *op. cit.,* p. 72.

25. *Declaration of the Rights of Man and Citizen,* pars. 2 and 3.

26. Camus, *op. cit.,* pp. 227–28.

27. Inter-American Peace Committee, *Report on the Relationship Between Violations of Human Rights or the Non-Exercise of Representative Democracy and the Political Tensions That Affect the Peace of the Hemisphere,* Document CIP-2-60 (Washington, D.C.: Pan American Union, 1960), p. 3.

28. For the situation in the Western hemisphere, see *Human Rights in the American States* (Washington, D.C.: Pan American Union, 1960).

29. Jesús de Galíndez, *La Era de Trujillo* (Santiago de Chile, 1956), p. 274.

30. Ciro Alegría, "Human Rights in Latin America," *The Annals of the American Academy of Political and Social Science,* CCXLIII (January, 1946), 87.

31. Henri Bergson, *The Two Sources of Morality and Religion,* trans. R. Ashley Audra and Cloudesley Brereton (New York: Doubleday & Co., 1935), Part 2.

32. See Karl Marx and Friedrich Engels, *The Communist Manifesto,* chap. ii.

33. Andrei Vishinsky, *The Law of the Soviet State,* trans. Hugh W. Babb (New York: The Macmillan Co., 1948).

34. Boris Tchechko, in *Human Rights, Comments and Interpretations,* pp. 169–70.

35. Sigmund Freud, *Civilization and Its Discontents*, trans. Joan Riviere (London: Hogarth Press, 1957), pp. 60–61.
36. *West Virginia State Board of Education* v. *Barnette*, 63 Sup. Ct. 1178, 1187; 319 U.S. 624, 642 (1943).

PART TWO: THE RIGHTS OF MAN—AND REPRESENTATIVE DEMOCRACY

1. See the International Declarations and Draft Conventions: American Declaration of the Rights and Duties of Man, Arts. 1, 17; Universal Declaration of Human Rights, Art. 3; Draft Convention on Human Rights of the Inter-American Council of Jurists, Arts. 2, 5; United Nations Draft Covenant on Civil and Political Rights, Arts. 6, 9; European Convention for the Protection of Human Rights and Fundamental Freedoms, Arts. 2, 5.
In the constitutions and legislation of the American states: Argentina—Civil Code, Arts. 51–70; Bolivia—Constitution, Art. 6; Civil Code, Art. 6; Brazil—Civil Code, Arts. 2–11; Chile—Civil Code, Arts. 55–57; Colombia—Civil Code, Arts. 73–74, 90–95; Costa Rica—Civil Code, Arts. 13–26; Cuba—Constitution, Art. 20; Civil Code, Arts. 29–32; Dominican Republic—Civil Code, Arts. 8, 11, 13, 488; Ecuador—Civil Code, Arts. 46–48, 66–67; El Salvador—Civil Code, Arts. 52–55, 72–76; Guatemala—Civil Code, Arts. 33–43; Haiti—Constitution, Arts. 6, 9; Honduras—Civil Code, Arts. 51–55; Mexico—Constitution, Art. 14; Civil Code, Arts. 2, 5, 12–14, 22–24; Nicaragua—Civil Code, Art. 1; Panama—Civil Code, Arts. 38–45; Paraguay—Civil Code, Arts. 51–70; Peru—Civil Code, Arts. 1–12; United States—5th, 13th, 14th, 15th Amendments to Constitution; Uruguay—Constitution, Arts. 7, 8; Civil Code, Arts. 4, 5, 21–23; Venezuela—Civil Code, Arts. 16–19, 26. For further details, see *Human Rights in the American States,* pp. 28 ff. and 54 ff.
2. *Human Rights, Comments and Interpretations,* p. 268. An exception is made for the right of society to impose the penalty of death for transgression of pre-existing, well-defined laws, with every possible protection afforded the accused to defend himself. See also *Human Rights in the American States,* pp. 28 ff.
3. Immanuel Kant, *The Philosophy of Law.*
4. Montesquieu, *op. cit.,* I, 183.
5. *Corpus Juris Secundum,* XVI, 1015.
6. It is contained in all the international declarations and draft conventions: American Declaration of the Rights and Duties of Man, Art.

8; Universal Declaration of Human Rights, Art. 13; Draft Convention on Human Rights of the Inter-American Council of Jurists, Art. 15; United Nations Draft Covenant on Civil and Political Rights, Art. 12.

In the American states, it is specifically included in all national constitutions: Argentina, Art. 14; Bolivia, Art. 6; Brazil, Art. 142; Chile, Art. 10(15); Colombia, Art. 23; Costa Rica, Arts. 22, 32; Cuba, Arts. 30, 41; Dominican Republic, Art. 8(12); Ecuador, Art. 187; El Salvador, Arts. 20, 154; Guatemala, Arts. 46–47; Haiti, Art. 15; Honduras, Arts. 30, 88; Mexico, Art. 11; Nicaragua, Arts. 59–60; Panama, Art. 27; Peru, Arts. 67–68; United States, 14th Amendment; Uruguay, Art. 37; Venezuela, Art. 64.

7. *Corpus Juris Secundum,* XVI, 987.

8. *Kent* v. *Dulles,* 78 Sup. Ct. 1113, 1118; 357 U.S. 116, 125 (1958).

9. Bolivia, Art. 111 (3, 4); Colombia, Art. 121; Costa Rica, Art. 121 (7); Cuba, Art. 41; Dominican Republic, Art. 114(8); El Salvador, Art. 176; Guatemala, Art. 77; Haiti, Art. 185; Honduras, Art. 163; Mexico, Art. 29; Nicaragua, Art. 197; Panama, Art. 52; Paraguay, Art. 52; Peru, Art. 70; Venezuela, Art. 241.

10. *New Introductory Lectures on Psychoanalysis,* trans. W. J. H. Sprott (New York: W. W. Norton, 1933), p. 233.

11. It is embodied in all the international declarations: American Declaration of the Rights and Duties of Man, Art. 18; Universal Declaration of Human Rights, Art. 8; European Convention for the Protection of Human Rights and Fundamental Freedoms, Art. 13. The draft U.N. covenants fail to refer to the protection of substantive due process, but it seems to be implied in their elaborate formulation of procedural due process. It is not, however, expressly provided for in many of the national constitutions of the American states. See *Human Rights in the American States,* especially pp. 34 ff. and 54 ff.

12. Lauterpacht, *op. cit.,* pp. 83–84.

13. *Snyder* v. *Massachusetts,* 54 Sup. Ct. 330, 332; 291 U.S. 97, 105 (1934).

14. *Palko* v. *Connecticut,* 58 Sup. Ct. 149, 152; 302 U.S. 319, 325 (1937).

15. *Wolf* v. *Colorado,* 69 Sup. Ct. 1359, 1361; 338 U.S. 25, 27 (1949).

16. This right has been acknowledged in all the international declarations of the rights of man and draft conventions on civil and political rights: American Declaration of the Rights and Duties of Man, Art. 25; Universal Declaration of Human Rights, Art. 9; Draft Convention on Human Rights of the Inter-American Council of Jurists, Art. 5; United Nations Draft Covenant on Civil and Political Rights, Art. 9; European Convention for the Protection of Human Rights and Fundamental Freedoms, Art. 5.

It is also contained in all the constitutions of the American states: Argentina, Art. 18; Bolivia, Art. 9; Brazil, Art. 141(20); Chile, Art. 13; Costa Rica, Art. 37; Cuba, Art. 27; Dominican Republic, Art. 8; Ecuador, Art. 187; El Salvador, Art. 166; Guatemala, Art. 43; Haiti, Art. 17; Honduras, Arts. 62, 69; Mexico, Art. 14; Nicaragua, Art. 39; Panama, Art. 22; Paraguay, Art. 26; Peru, Art. 56; United States, 14th Amendment; Uruguay, Art. 15; and Venezuela, Art. 60.

17. Blackstone's *Commentaries*, IV.

18. American Bar Association, "Memorandum on the Detention of Arrested Persons and Their Production Before a Committing Magistrate," cited in: Zechariah Chafee, Jr. (ed.), *Documents on Fundamental Human Rights* (Cambridge, Mass.: Harvard University Press, 1951), II, 483, 488.

19. Inter-American Commission on Human Rights, *Report on the Situation of Political Prisoners and Their Relatives in Cuba*, OEA/Ser.L/V/II.7 (Washington, D.C.: Pan American Union, 1963).

20. *McNabb* v. *U.S.*, 63 Sup. Ct. 608; 318 U.S. 332 (1943).

21. Art. 1, sec. 9. See also *Ex Parte Milligan*, 4 Wallace 2 (1866).

22. It has been incorporated in all the international declarations and draft conventions: American Declaration of the Rights and Duties of Man, Arts. 9, 10; Universal Declaration of Human Rights, Art. 12; Draft Convention on Human Rights of the Inter-American Council of Jurists, Art. 8; European Convention for the Protection of Human Rights and Fundamental Freedoms, Art. 8; United Nations Draft Covenant on Civil and Political Rights, Art. 17. Not all the constitutions of the American states contain it in express terms. See *Human Rights in the American States*, pp. 71 ff.

23. *Olmstead* v. *U.S.*, 48 Sup. Ct. 564; 227 U.S. 438, 478 (1928).

24. *Wolf* v. *Colorado*, 69 Sup. Ct. 1359, 1361; 338 U.S. 25, 27 (1949).

25. Argentina, Art. 23; Bolivia, Arts. 110–14; Brazil, Arts. 206–15; Chile, Arts. 44, 72; Colombia, Art. 121; Costa Rica, Art. 121; Cuba, Arts. 41, 42; Dominican Republic, Arts. 114, 128; Ecuador, Arts. 94–99; El Salvador, Arts. 176–79; Guatemala, Arts. 77, 78; Haiti, Arts. 185, 186; Honduras, Arts. 163–72; Mexico, Art. 29; Nicaragua, Arts. 196, 197; Panama, Arts. 52, 53; Paraguay, Art. 52; Peru, Art. 70; Uruguay, Arts. 31, 168; Venezuela, Arts. 240, 244.

26. A. Powell Davies, as quoted in William O. Douglas, *The Right of the People* (New York: Doubleday, 1958), p. 90.

27. See American Declaration of the Rights and Duties of Man, Preamble; Universal Declaration of Human Rights, Art. 1.

28. This principle is fundamental in all international formulations of basic human rights: American Declaration of the Rights and Duties of Man, Art. 2; Universal Declaration of Human Rights, Arts. 2, 7; Draft Convention on Human Rights of the Inter-American Council of Jurists, Arts. 17, 18; United Nations Draft Covenant on Civil and Political Rights, Arts. 14, 24; European Convention for the Protection of Human Rights and Fundamental Freedoms, Art. 14.

It is also embodied in the constitutions of the nations of the Western hemisphere: Argentina, Art. 16; Brazil, Art. 141; Chile, Art. 10; Costa

Rica, Art. 33; Ecuador, Art. 169; El Salvador, Art. 150; Guatemala, Arts. 40, 42; Honduras, Art. 57; Mexico, Arts. 1, 12; Panama, Art. 21; Peru, Art. 23; United States, 14th Amendment; Uruguay, Arts. 8, 9. For further details, see *Human Rights in the American States*, pp. 30 ff.

29. International Commission of Jurists, *The Rule of Law in a Free Society*, Report of the International Congress of Jurists, New Delhi, January 5–10, 1959, p. 212.

30. *Yick Wo* v. *Hopkins*, 6 Sup. Ct. 1064, 1070; 118 U.S. 356, 369 (1886).

31. *Corpus Juris Secundum*, XVIA, 297–99.

32. Harold Laski, in *Human Rights, Comments and Interpretations*, p. 80.

33. *Oyama* v. *California*, 68 Sup. Ct. 269, 275; 332 U.S. 633, 646 (1948).

34. Justice Black's dissent in *American Communications Association* v. *Douds*, 70 Sup. Ct. 674; 339 U.S. 382, 448 (1950).

35. *Pierre* v. *State of Louisiana*, 59 Sup. Ct. 536, 539; 306 U.S. 354, 358 (1934).

36. *Civilization and Its Discontents*, p. 61.

37. These rights are contained in all the international declarations and drafts: American Declaration of the Rights and Duties of Man, Arts. 21, 22; Universal Declaration of Human Rights, Art. 20; Draft Convention on Human Rights of the Inter-American Council of Jurists, Arts. 12, 13; United Nations Draft Covenant on Civil and Political Rights, Arts. 20, 21; European Convention for the Protection of Human Rights and Fundamental Freedoms, Art. 11.

They are also elaborately provided for in the constitutions of all the American nations: Argentina, Art. 14; Bolivia, Art. 6; Brazil, Arts. 141, 209; Chile, Art. 10; Colombia, Art. 46; Costa Rica, Arts. 25–26, 60–62; Cuba, Arts. 37, 69–70, 102–3; Dominican Republic, Art. 8; Ecuador, Art. 187(13); El Salvador, Arts. 145, 160; Guatemala, Arts. 53–54; Haiti, Arts. 31–32; Honduras, Art. 85; Mexico, Art. 9; Nicaragua, Arts. 115–16; Panama, Arts. 39–40, 67; Paraguay, Arts. 19, 32; Peru, Arts. 27, 62; United States, 1st Amendment; Uruguay, Arts. 38–39, 57; Venezuela, Arts. 70, 71. See also *Human Rights in the American States*, pp. 68 ff.

38. *U.S.* v. *Cruikshank*, 92 U.S. 542, 552 (1875).

39. *Sweezy* v. *New Hampshire*, 77 Sup. Ct. 1203, 1212; 354 U.S. 234, 250 (1957).

40. Antonio Caso, *La Persona Humana y el Estado Totalitario* (Mexico City, 1941), pp. 142–43. Translation in Crawford, *op. cit.*, p. 288.

41. Draft Convention on Human Rights of the Inter-American Council of Jurists, Arts. 12, 13; United Nations Draft Covenant on Civil and Political Rights, Arts. 20, 21; European Convention for the Protection of Human Rights and Fundamental Freedoms, Art. 11.

42. Douglas, *op. cit.*, p. 59.

43. Annotations on the Text of the Draft International Covenants on Human Rights, United Nations, General Assembly, 10th Session (New York, 1955). Official Records, Document A/2929, p. 54.

44. Drost, *op. cit.*, p. 67.

45. In the constitutions of the American states, sixteen nations have seen fit to include it, as follows: Argentina, Art. 14; Brazil, Art. 141(37); Chile, Art. 10(6); Colombia, Art. 45; Costa Rica, Art. 27; Cuba, Art. 36; Ecuador, Art. 187(12); El Salvador, Art. 162; Guatemala, Art. 52; Haiti, Art. 33; Mexico, Art. 8; Nicaragua, Art. 117; Panama, Art. 42; Paraguay, Art. 19; Peru, Art. 26; Uruguay, Art. 30.

46. Their inseparability is acknowledged in all the recent international declarations and draft conventions: American Declaration of the Rights and Duties of Man, Art. 4; Universal Declaration of Human Rights, Art. 19; Draft Convention on Human Rights of the Inter-American Council of Jurists, Art. 10; United Nations Draft Covenant on Civil and Political Rights, Arts. 18, 19; Draft Convention on the Effective Exercise of Representative Democracy, Art. 5; European Convention for the Protection of Human Rights and Fundamental Freedoms, Arts. 9, 10.

47. In the American states, all constitutions make provision for it: Argentina, Art. 14; Bolivia, Art. 6; Brazil, Art. 141(5); Chile, Art. 10(3); Colombia, Art. 42; Costa Rica, Arts. 28, 29; Cuba, Art. 33; Dominican Republic, Art. 8(7); Ecuador, Art. 187(11); El Salvador, Art. 158; Guatemala, Art. 57; Haiti, Art. 26; Honduras, Arts. 81, 83; Mexico, Arts. 6, 7; Nicaragua, Art. 113; Panama, Art. 38; Paraguay, Art. 19; Peru, Arts. 59, 63; United States, 1st and 14th Amendments; Uruguay, Art. 29; Venezuela, Art. 66.

48. *Palko v. Connecticut,* 58 Sup. Ct. 149, 152; 302 U.S. 319, 327 (1937).

49. Annotations on the Text of the Draft International Covenants on Human Rights, p. 50.

50. Declaration of Santiago, Fifth Meeting of Consultation of Ministers of Foreign Affairs, Santiago de Chile, 1959. See also Emergency Advisory Committee for Political Defense, *Legislation for the Political Defense of the American Republics* (Montevideo, 1947), II, 4.

51. *Dennis et al.* v. *U.S.,* 71 Sup. Ct. 857, 905; 341 U.S. 494, 584 (1951).

52. Meiklejohn, *op. cit.*, pp. 25–27.

53. *Whitney* v. *California,* 47 Sup. Ct. 641, 648; 274 U.S. 357, 375 (1927).

54. Herodotus vii, par. 10.

55. Chung-Shu Lo, in *Human Rights, Comments and Interpretations,* p. 189.

56. Journal of the Continental Congress (1904 ed.), I, 104, 108. See also *Thornhill* v. *Alabama,* 60 Sup. Ct. 736, 744; 310 U.S. 88, 102 (1940).

57. Zechariah Chafee, Jr., *Free Speech in the United States* (2d ed.; Cambridge, Mass.: Harvard University Press, 1948), p. 18.

58. Meiklejohn, *op. cit.*, pp. 93–94.

59. *New York University Law Review,* XXXVII (1962), 549, 559.

60. Douglas, *op. cit.,* p. 34.

61. Samuel Johnson, as quoted in *ibid.,* p. 45.

62. *Human Rights, Comments and Interpretations,* p. 271. Such limitations have also been acknowledged in all international declarations and draft conventions.

63. *DeJonge* v. *Oregon,* 57 Sup. Ct. 255; 299 U.S. 353, 364–65 (1937).

64. Dissent in *Abrams* v. *United States,* 40 Sup. Ct. 17; 250 U.S. 616 (1919). For a summary of the numerous problems presented in the interpretation of the "clear and present danger" test, see Meiklejohn, *op. cit.,* pp. 47 ff.

65. Article 26.

66. Annotations on the Text of the Draft International Covenant on Human Rights, pp. 52, 64.

67. For a discussion and review of the doctrine of prior restraint, see *Near* v. *Minnesota,* 51 Sup. Ct. 625; 283 U.S. 697 (1931).

68. Annotations on the Text of the Draft International Covenant on Human Rights, p. 42.

69. Montesquieu, *op. cit.* I, 183–84, 185.

70. See American Declaration of the Rights and Duties of Man, Arts. 18, 26; Universal Declaration of Human Rights, Arts. 8, 10; Draft Convention on Human Rights of the Inter-American Council of Jurists, Art. 6; United Nations Draft Covenant on Civil and Political Rights, Art. 14; European Convention for the Protection of Human Rights and Fundamental Freedoms, Arts. 6, 13.

In the constitutions of the American nations, note Argentina, Art. 18; Bolivia, Art. 14; Brazil, Art. 141(26, 27); Chile, Art. 12; Costa Rica, Art. 35; Cuba, Art. 28; Ecuador, Art. 169; El Salvador, Art. 169; Guatemala, Art. 60; Honduras, Art. 78; Mexico, Art. 13; Paraguay, Art. 26; Peru, Art. 57; Venezuela, Art. 69.

See also comments in *Human Rights in the American States,* pp. 37 ff. See Resolution I, No. 5, Declaration of Santiago, Fifth Meeting of Consultation of Ministers of Foreign Affairs, Santiago de Chile, 1959.

71. *Human Rights in the American States,* p. 38.

72. Magna Carta, par. 40.

73. St. Augustine, *The City of God,* Book IV, chap. iv.

74. *Truax* v. *Corrigan,* 42 Sup. Ct. 124, 129; 257 U.S. 312, 332 (1921).

75. Draft Convention on Human Rights of the Inter-American Council of Jurists, Art. 6; United Nations Draft Covenant on Civil and Political Rights, Art. 14; European Convention for the Protection of Human Rights and Fundamental Freedoms, Art. 6.

76. Quoted by Justice Black in *In re Oliver,* 68 Sup. Ct. 499; 333 U.S. 257 (1948).

77. *The Rule of Law in a Free Society*, p. 247.

78. *Corpus Juris Secundum*, XVIA, 140.

79. It is included in the international declarations and draft conventions: American Declaration of the Rights and Duties of Man, Arts. 25, 26; Universal Declaration of Human Rights, Arts. 2, 11; Draft Convention on Human Rights of the Inter-American Council of Jurists, Arts. 2, 7; United Nations Draft Covenant on Civil and Political Rights, Art. 15; European Convention for the Protection of Human Rights and Fundamental Freedoms, Art. 7.

80. *The Rule of Law in a Free Society*, p. 211.

81. *Brown v. Board of Education*, 74 Sup. Ct. 686, 691; 347 U.S. 483, 493 (1954).

82. José do Manoel Bomfim, *A America latina* (Rio de Janeiro, 1905), p. 429; cited in Crawford, *op. cit.*, p. 202.

83. *On Liberty*.

84. As quoted in Alegría, *op. cit.*, p. 89.

85. See American Declaration of the Rights and Duties of Man, Art. 12; Universal Declaration of Human Rights, Art. 26; Draft Convention on Human Rights of the Inter-American Council of Jurists, Arts. 27, 28, 30; United Nations Draft Covenant on Social and Economic Rights, Art. 14; Protocol to European Convention, Art. 2.

It is also provided for in the constitutions of the various American nations: Argentina, Arts. 5, 14, 67(16); Bolivia, Arts, 6, 186–89; Brazil, Arts. 166–75; Chile, Art. 10(7); Colombia, Art. 41; Costa Rica, Arts. 77–89; Cuba, Arts. 47–59; Dominican Republic, Art. 8(6); Ecuador, Arts. 171–73, 174(c); El Salvador, Arts. 197–205; Guatemala, Arts. 95–111; Haiti, Arts. 29, 166–70; Honduras, Arts. 89, 135–53; Mexico, Arts. 3, 31(I); Nicaragua, Arts. 77, 78, 83, 98, 109; Panama, Arts. 77–91, 94, 96; Paraguay, Arts. 10, 11, 19; Peru, Arts. 71–83; Uruguay, Arts. 34, 41, 68–71; Venezuela, Art. 78. See also *Human Rights in the American States*, pp. 79 ff.

86. Resolution XI, Inter-American Conference on Problems of War and Peace, Mexico City, 1945.

PART THREE: THE DUTIES OF MAN AND LIMITATIONS ON HUMAN RIGHTS

1. Mahatma Gandhi, Letter to Julian Huxley, Director-General of UNESCO, in *Human Rights, Comments and Interpretations*, p. 18.

2. Drost, *op. cit.*, p. 233.

3. Annotations on the Text of the Draft International Covenants on Human Rights, p. 54, par. 143. Provisions are made in the constitutions of all the American nations. See *Human Rights in the American States*, pp. 69, 76–77. Similar provisions are found in the international declara-

tions and conventions: American Declaration of the Rights and Duties of Man, Art. 28; Universal Declaration of Human Rights, Art. 29; Draft Convention on Human Rights of the Inter-American Council of Jurists, Arts. 10, 12, 13, 19; United Nations Draft Covenant on Civil and Political Rights, Arts. 4, 19, 20, 21; European Convention for the Protection of Human Rights and Fundamental Freedoms, Arts. 8, 10, 11, 15.

In the Statute of the Inter-American Commission on Human Rights, it is stated in Article 10: "the Commission shall act . . . and bear in mind particularly that . . . the rights of each man are limited by the rights of others, by the security of all, and by the just demands of the general welfare and advancement of democracy."

4. *Human Rights, Comments and Interpretations*, pp. 156–57.

5. Cited in Crawford, *op. cit.*, p. 249.

6. It is contained in the international documents: Draft Convention on Human Rights of the Inter-American Council of Jurists, Art. 19; United Nations Draft Covenant on Civil and Political Rights, Art. 4; European Convention for the Protection of Human Rights and Fundamental Freedoms, Art. 15.

7. Annotations on the Text of the Draft International Covenants on Human Rights, p. 23, par. 37.

8. For a résumé of this history, see Clodomiro Bravo Michell and Nissim Sharim Paz, *Restricciones a las Libertades Públicas* (Santiago de Chile, 1958), pp. 122 ff.

9. William W. Pierson and Federico G. Gil, *Governments of Latin America* (New York: McGraw-Hill, 1957), p. 165. The authors state that every Latin American constitution grants such power.

10. See the constitutions of Colombia, Art. 121; and Haiti, Arts. 185, 186.

11. Inter-American Commission on Human Rights, *Preliminary Study of the State of Siege and the Protection of Human Rights in the Americas*, OEA/Ser.L/V/II.8 (Washington, D.C.: Pan American Union, 1963).

12. See the emphasis given to the danger in Resolution I, Pt. 4(c), Eighth Meeting of Consultation of Ministers of Foreign Affairs (Punta del Este, 1962).

13. Quoted in Douglas, *op. cit.*, p. 211.

14. *The Federalist Papers*, No. VIII.

15. Emergency Consultative Committee for the Political Defense of the Hemisphere, *Legislación para la Defensa Política en las Repúblicas Americanas* (Montevideo: Pan American Union, 1947), p. 82.

16. *Ibid.*, Art. 1, Sec. 9.

17. *Thomas v. Collin*, 65 Sup. Ct. 315, 322; 323 U.S. 516, 530 (1945).

18. *Ex Parte Milligan*, 4 Wallace 2 (1866).

19. Douglas, *op. cit.*, pp. 201–2.

PART FOUR: THE ROAD AHEAD AND THE
ROLE OF INTERNATIONAL ORGANIZATION

1. Pan American Union, *Minutes of the Meeting of the Council of the OAS*, Washington, D.C., May 28, 1958, p. 14.
2. Inter-American Juridical Committee, *Study on the Juridical Relationship Between Respect for Human Rights and the Exercise of Democracy*, Document CIJ-52 (Washington, D.C.: Pan American Union, 1960), pp. 15–16.
3. *Ibid.* p. 11.
4. First Symposium on Representative Democracy, Santo Domingo, December, 1962, *Final Report* (Washington, D.C.: Pan American Union, 1963), pp. 12–13.